CAFÉ
KITCHEN

CAFÉ KITCHEN

RELAXED FOOD
FOR FEEDING
FRIENDS AT HOME

SHELAGH RYAN

Lantana CAFÉ

photography by Kate Whitaker

RYLAND PETERS & SMALL
LONDON • NEW YORK

Senior Designer Megan Smith
Commissioning Editors
Stephanie Milner and Céline Hughes
Head of Production Patricia
Harrington
Art Director Leslie Harrington
Editorial Director Julia Charles
Publisher Cindy Richards

Prop Stylist Tony Hutchinson
Food Stylist Lucy McKelvie
Assistant Food Stylist Ellie Jarvis
Indexer Sandra Shotter

First published in 2014 by
Ryland Peters & Small
20–21 Jockey's Fields,
London WC1R 4BW
and
519 Broadway, 5th Floor,
New York NY 10012
www.rylandpeters.com

NOTES

• Both British (Metric) and
American (Imperial plus US cups)
measurements and ingredients are
included in these recipes for your
convenience, however it is
important to work with one set of
measurements and not alternate
between the two within a recipe.
Spellings are primarily British.
• All spoon measurements are level
unless otherwise specified.
• All eggs are medium (UK) or large
(US), unless specified as large, in
which case US extra-large should
be used. Uncooked or partially
cooked eggs should not be served
to the very old, frail, young children,
pregnant women or those with
compromised immune systems.
• When a recipe calls for the grated
zest of citrus fruit, buy unwaxed
fruit and wash well before using.
If you can only find treated fruit,
scrub well in warm, soapy water
before using.
• Ovens should be preheated
to the specified temperatures.
We recommend using an oven
thermometer. If using a fan-assisted
oven, adjust temperatures according
to the manufacturer's instructions.
• Sterilize preserving jars before
use. Wash them in hot, soapy water
and rinse in boiling water. Place in a
large saucepan and then cover with
hot water. With the lid on, bring the
water to the boil and continue
boiling for 15 minutes. Turn off the
heat, then leave the jars in the hot
water until just before they are to
be filled. Invert the jars onto clean
paper towels to dry. Sterilize the
lids for 5 minutes, by boiling, or
according to the manufacturer's
instructions. Jars should be filled
and sealed while they are still hot.

CONTENTS

INTRODUCTION

Cafés are not fast food fuel stops, nor are they fancy, special occasion restaurants. They are casual, relaxed places that form part of our daily and weekly routines – somewhere to stop in for your morning coffee and breakfast on the way to work, to catch up with friends for brunch at the weekend, or to indulge in a piece of cake and a pot of tea on a rainy afternoon. They should be warm, comforting spaces that serve the type of food that we want to cook in our own kitchens; unpretentious and simply cooked dishes using fresh, quality ingredients.

I love it when customers in our cafés ask for a recipe or I overhear a table discussing their meal, trying to put their finger on a particular ingredient so they can recreate the dish themselves. Imitation is the sincerest form of flattery and many of the recipes in this book are ones that our customers love and have repeatedly requested. However, this is not intended to be a 'restaurant cookbook'. The point of this book is to demonstrate that there is no magic behind food prepared in a restaurant or café. Eating at your own kitchen table can be just as good, if not better, than eating out. Sure, a trained chef may use techniques to create extraordinary dishes that are beyond the capabilities of most amateur cooks, but delicious food can also be very simply prepared in your own home.

This book is full of easy-to-follow recipes for enthusiastic eaters who enjoy the process of cooking, and expect more from food than simply for it to be fast, cheap and filling. There are recipes for every meal of the day, some that are quick to prepare and others for when you have the luxury of time. I always like to make something at the weekend that I can eat later in the week when I know I'm going to be busy and have less energy to cook. I actually think Caponata (page 128) tastes better a day or two after it is made; a dish that can be transformed into many meals: the perfect base for baked eggs, stirred through pasta with some soft feta cheese or served as an accompaniment to grilled fish or roast lamb.

Adaptability is an essential part of the way I think about food. I encourage you to be creative with the recipes, adapt them to suit the occasion and the season. Mix and match them at will. The Baked Ricotta on page 105 could be served with a simple tomato salad if you don't have time to make the Aubergine, Currant & Pine Nut Relish. The Mango Salsa for the Spicy Pork Burgers on page 98 also tastes delicious with grilled chicken or with fishcakes, and the poached cherries for the Cherry Muffins on page 18 are perfect for Eton Mess when fresh berries aren't in season.

I hope these recipes will provide you with inspiration for many meals, whether you are cooking for yourself, your family or having friends over. Your kitchen table may become your new favourite place to eat.

BREAKFAST & BRUNCH

Making muesli is one of the comforting rituals in my life. I love filling my shopping bag with oats, barley, nuts, seeds, and dried fruit, mixing all the ingredients together and slowly toasting them in the oven. Store it in a glass jar on the kitchen counter to admire: a breakfast of champions.

TOASTED MUESLI WITH BAKED RHUBARB

100 ml/$\frac{1}{3}$ cup sunflower oil

$\frac{1}{2}$ teaspoon pure vanilla extract

125 ml/$\frac{1}{3}$ cup clear honey

125 ml/$\frac{1}{2}$ cup maple syrup

$\frac{1}{4}$ teaspoon ground cinnamon

500 g/$2\frac{1}{2}$ cups jumbo rolled oats

150 g/$1\frac{1}{2}$ cups rolled barley flakes

70 g/$\frac{2}{3}$ cup wheatgerm

50 g/$\frac{2}{3}$ cup shredded/desiccated coconut

125 g/$1\frac{1}{4}$ cup almonds

100 g/1 cup pecans

125 g/scant 1 cup sunflower seeds

100 g/$\frac{2}{3}$ cup pumpkin seeds

10 g/1 tablespoon sesame seeds

250 g/$1\frac{2}{3}$ cup (dark) raisins

200 g/$1\frac{1}{2}$ cup dried dates, halved

Greek yogurt, to serve

BAKED RHUBARB

500 g/5 cups rhubarb, trimmed and cut into 5-cm/2-inch pieces

2 tablespoons caster/granulated sugar

freshly squeezed juice and grated zest of 1 orange

2 baking sheets, greased and lined with baking parchment

sterilized, glass jars with airtight lids (optional)

SERVES 10

Preheat the oven to 130°C (250°F) Gas $\frac{1}{2}$.

Pour the oil, vanilla, honey, syrup and cinnamon into a saucepan or pot set over a gentle heat and stir to combine.

Mix together all the remaining ingredients, except the (dark) raisins, dates and yogurt in a large mixing bowl. Pour over the hot oil mixture and stir well to ensure everything is well coated.

Spread the mixture evenly onto the prepared baking sheets and bake in the preheated oven for 30–45 minutes. Stir the mixture at regular intervals and cook until evenly golden and dry. Remove from the oven and set aside to cool completely before adding the reserved (dark) raisins and dates.

To make the Baked Rhubarb, preheat the oven to 150°C (300°F) Gas 2. Place the rhubarb in a baking pan that is big enough to hold it in a single layer. Sprinkle over the sugar, orange juice and zest, and gently mix together. Cover with foil and bake in the preheated oven for 30–45 minutes, until the rhubarb is just soft. Remove from the oven and set aside to cool completely before serving with the toasted muesli and Greek yogurt.

Store any leftover muesli and baked rhubarb in separate airtight containers or sterilized glass jars fitted with airtight lids. The muesli will keep at room temperature for up to 2 weeks and the rhubarb should be kept in the fridge for 3–5 days.

A fantastic alternative to porridge for summer, this is one of those recipes that can be modified ad infinitum. Try substituting the apple juice with orange or cranberry, add pumpkin seeds, macadamia nuts, dried apricots or any dried or poached fruit.

BIRCHER MUESLI WITH FRESH BERRIES

250 g/1¼ cups jumbo rolled oats
30 g/⅓ cup (dark) raisins
375 ml/1½ cups apple juice
30 g/⅓ cup whole almonds
freshly squeezed juice and grated zest of ½ lemon
1 apple or pear, coarsely grated
125 ml/½ cup yogurt

TO SERVE
mixed fresh berries
clear honey

a baking sheet, greased and lined with baking parchment

SERVES 4

Place the oats and raisins in a large mixing bowl and pour over the apple juice. Cover with clingfilm/plastic wrap and chill in the fridge for at least an hour, preferably overnight.

Preheat the oven to 180°C (350°F) Gas 4.

Scatter the almonds onto the prepared baking sheet and toast in the preheated oven for about 10 minutes.

Remove from the oven and set aside to cool before chopping to a rough texture.

Remove the soaked oat mixture from the fridge. Uncover and add the lemon juice and zest, chopped toasted almonds and grated apple or pear. Stir to combine.

Add the yogurt, a little at a time, stirring after each addition to your desired consistency.

Serve in bowls with fresh berries on top and a drizzle of honey.

The secret to perfectly poached fruit is to poach each type of fruit individually as each has a different cooking time. You want the fruit to hold its shape so try to use fruit that is still quite firm and take care not to overcook it. The magic ingredient in our poached fruit is verjuice, a juice made from unfermented grapes, but if you can't find this, use a combination of apple and lemon juice or a dry wine.

VERJUICE POACHED FRUIT

500 ml/2 cups verjuice (or 500 ml/2 cups apple juice mixed with the freshly squeezed juice of 1 lemon)
½ vanilla bean/pod, sliced lengthways
a pinch of saffron
1 cinnamon stick
250 g/1¼ cups caster/granulated sugar
freshly squeezed juice of ½ orange, plus the skin
750 g/3 cups (about 5 medium) peeled, cored and quartered pears
300 g/3 cups (about 2 medium) peeled, cored and quartered green apples
100 g/scant ⅔ cup (about 4) stoned/pitted and quartered plums
250 g/2½ cups rhubarb, trimmed and cut into 4-cm/1½-inch pieces

TO SERVE
150 g/1½ cups blueberries
Greek yogurt

SERVES 6

Pour 750 ml/3 cups of water with the verjuice (or substitute) into a heavy-bottomed saucepan or pot set over a medium–high heat. Add the vanilla pod/bean, including the seeds scraped with back of a sharp knife, the saffron, cinnamon and sugar. Squeeze the juice from the ½ of the orange into the pan and put the squeezed skin in too. Bring the liquid to the boil, then reduce the heat and simmer for 15 minutes.

Add the quartered pears to the simmering poaching liquor, cover the surface with a circle of baking parchment to keep the fruit submerged and cook for about 15 minutes. The pears should be tender and still hold their shape. Remove the fruit from the pan and transfer to a large mixing bowl. Repeat with the other fruits, poaching each separately for the following times: the apples for 8–10 minutes, the plums for 5 minutes and the rhubarb for 3 minutes.

When all the fruit is cooked, increase the heat and simmer the liquor for a further 5 minutes to reduce it to a syrup. Remove the pan from the heat and let the syrup cool completely before pouring it over the poached fruit.

Remove and discard the cinnamon stick, vanilla pod/bean and orange skin if you like, but I like to keep them in for decoration.

Add the blueberries just before serving – they add a nice little burst of freshness – and serve the fruit in bowls with some syrup drizzled over and a dollop of Greek yogurt.

One of the best reasons to make your own jam/jelly is that you can make it how you like it. A lot of jam/jelly recipes use equal amounts of sugar and fruit which I find too sweet so I use half as much sugar – it's still sweet without obliterating the taste of the fruit.

APPLE & GINGER JAM

750 g/7½ cups (about 5 medium) green apples, peeled, cored and diced

freshly squeezed juice and grated zest of 1 lemon

375 g/scant 2 cups caster/granulated sugar

30 g/¼ cup (2 balls) stem ginger, diced, plus 3 tablespoons syrup

1 teaspoon ground ginger

20 g/3 tablespoons peeled and finely grated fresh ginger

sterilized, glass jars with airtight lids

MAKES 1 LITRE (36 OZ.)/4 CUPS

MIXED BERRY JAM

500 g/5 cups mixed fresh berries

250 g/2¼ cups caster/granulated sugar

peeled zest of 1 lemon, cut into wide strips

MAKES 500 ML (18 OZ.)/2 CUPS

Place the apples, lemon juice and zest in a saucepan or pot set over a gentle heat and warm through until apples are soft. Add the sugar, stem, ground and fresh ginger. Stir to combine and cook until the sugar has dissolved. It is important to dissolve the sugar before the jam reaches boiling point otherwise it may not set.

Increase the heat and bring the jam to the boil. Let it boil rapidly for 2 minutes then reduce the heat and simmer for 10 minutes, stirring occasionally, until the jam is thick. You should be able to run a spoon along the bottom of the pan and leave a path for a few seconds before the jam runs into it.

While still warm, spoon the jam into sterilized, glass jars. Carefully tap them on the counter to get rid of any air pockets, wipe clean and tightly screw on the lids. Turn the jars upside down and leave until completely cold. Store unopened in a cool, dark place for up to 6 months or in the fridge for up to 2 months. Once opened, store in the fridge and use within 2 weeks.

VARIATION

To make Mixed Berry Jam, place all of the ingredients in a saucepan or pot set over a gentle heat, stir to combine, cook and store as above, removing the lemon peel before spooning the jam into jars.

Who doesn't love a freshly baked muffin, especially when they are bursting with fruit so you can convince yourself that they are healthy?

RASPBERRY & APPLE
MUFFINS

1 egg
180 g/1 scant cup golden caster/pure cane sugar
70 g/5 tablespoons unsalted butter, melted and cooled
180 ml/¾ cup milk
grated zest of 1 lemon
1 teaspoon pure vanilla extract
100 g/1 cup (about 1 small) peeled, cored and diced green apple

125g/1 generous cup fresh raspberries, plus 4 halved to garnish
270 g/2 cups plus 1 tablespoon self-raising/rising flour
½ teaspoon baking powder
¼ teaspoon salt
icing/confectioners' sugar, to dust

a 12-hole muffin pan lined with 8 paper cases

MAKES 8

Preheat the oven to 170°C (325°F) Gas 3.

Beat the egg and golden caster/pure cane sugar together in a large mixing bowl until light and a pale cream colour. Add the cooled melted butter, milk, lemon zest and vanilla, and mix until combined. Stir in the apple and raspberries, then sift in the flour, baking powder and salt. Gently fold the mixture with a large spoon – take care not to over beat the mixture and stop as soon as it comes together, even if it is still lumpy.

Divide the batter between the muffin cases and place a raspberry half on top of each.

Bake in the preheated oven for 30 minutes, until light brown and a skewer inserted into the middle comes out clean.

Dust with icing/confectioners' sugar and serve straight from the oven. The muffins are best eaten on the day of baking but will last for up to 2 days if stored in an airtight container.

CHERRY MUFFINS

150 g/1 generous cup pitted/stoned cherries
½ teaspoon caster/granulated sugar
1 teaspoon pure vanilla extract
1 egg
180 g/1 scant cup golden caster/pure cane sugar
1 teaspoon pure vanilla extract
70 g/5 tablespoons unsalted butter, melted and cooled

180 ml/¾ cup milk
270 g/2 cups plus 2 tablespoons self-raising/rising flour
½ teaspoon baking powder
¼ teaspoon salt
icing/confectioners' sugar to dust

a 12-hole muffin pan lined with 8 paper cases

MAKES 8

Begin by poaching the cherries. Place them with the caster/granulated sugar, vanilla and 2 tablespoons of water in a small saucepan or pot set over a gentle heat. Warm until the sugar dissolves, swirling the pan to coat the cherries. Simmer for 1 minute then remove from the heat.

Preheat the oven to 170°C (325°F) Gas 3.

Beat the egg and golden caster/pure cane sugar together in a large mixing bowl until light and a pale cream colour. Add the cooled melted butter and milk, and mix until combined. Stir in the poached cherries, then sift in the flour, baking powder and salt. Gently fold the mixture with a large spoon – take care not to over beat the mixture and stop as soon as it comes together, even if it is still lumpy.

Divide the batter between the muffin cases and bake in the preheated oven for 30 minutes, until light brown and a skewer inserted into the middle comes out clean.

Dust with icing/confectioners' sugar and serve straight from the oven.

Banana bread is absolutely delicious on its own or toasted with butter but if you want an indulgent start to the day, try it with this beautiful Raspberry Labne. Labne is a strained yogurt which has a consistency somewhere between cream cheese and yogurt. The longer you leave it, the firmer it becomes so play around with the consistency.

BANANA BREAD WITH RASPBERRY LABNE

125 g/1 stick unsalted butter, softened
250 g/1¼ cups caster/granulated sugar
2 large eggs, beaten
1 teaspoon pure vanilla extract
250g/2 cups plain/all-purpose flour
2 teaspoons baking powder
4 very ripe bananas, mashed

RASPBERRY LABNE
150 g/1 generous cup fresh or frozen raspberries
100 g/½ cup caster/granulated sugar
500 g/2 cups Greek yogurt
1 teaspoon pure vanilla extract

a 900-g/2-lb loaf pan, greased and lined with baking parchment
2 fine mesh sieves/strainers, 1 lined with several layers of muslin/cheesecloth

MAKES 8 SLICES AND SERVES 4

Preheat the oven to 180°C (350°F) Gas 4.

Beat the butter and caster/granulated sugar together in a large mixing bowl until light, fluffy and a pale cream colour. Gradually beat in the eggs, one at a time, before adding the vanilla.

In a separate bowl, sift together the flour and baking powder.

Gently fold the mashed bananas into the wet mixture a little at a time, alternating with the sifted flour mixture so that the mixture doesn't split.

Transfer the banana batter to the prepared loaf pan, then bake in the preheated oven for 20 minutes.

Reduce the oven temperature to 160°C (325°F) Gas 3 and cook for a further 40–45 minutes until golden brown, firm to the touch and a skewer inserted into the middle comes out clean.

Set aside to cool in the pan for 5 minutes then turn out onto a wire rack to cool completely.

To make the Raspberry Labne, place 50 g/½ cup of the raspberries in a small saucepan or pot with the sugar and 100 ml/scant ½ cup of water. Set over a gentle heat and simmer until it reduces by one-third.

Remove from the heat and strain through the unlined sieve/strainer set over a mixing bowl. Discard the raspberry pulp, cover the syrup and set aside to cool completely.

Add the yogurt, cooled raspberry syrup, vanilla and remaining raspberries, and mix together. Pour the mixture into the lined sieve/strainer set over a mixing bowl. Draw the cloth together, twist the gathered cloth to form a tight ball and tie the ends with kitchen string. Suspend the wrapped labne over the bowl and set in the fridge for 12–24 hours. Discard the drained water and transfer the labne to a bowl, ready to serve with slices of banana bread.

Fishcakes are a complete meal — fish and herby potatoes in one convenient parcel. They need only a simple salad on the side. Poached eggs are optional but the creamy yolk mixed with potato is pretty special, and it is brunch after all.

SMOKED HADDOCK FISHCAKES WITH POACHED EGGS & DILL MAYO

700 g/1¾ lbs. (about 4 large) Maris Piper, King Edward or other floury potatoes
300 ml/1¼ cups milk
1 bay leaf
400 g/14 oz. undyed smoked haddock
25 g/½ cup chives, finely chopped
20 g/scant ½ cup dill, finely chopped
25 g/2 tablespoons melted butter
sea salt and freshly ground black pepper
1 egg, lightly beaten, plus 6 for poaching
vegetable oil, for frying

DILL MAYO
200 ml/¾ cup mayonnaise
1 tablespoon chopped dill
½ teaspoon grated lemon zest
1 tablespoon lemon juice

TO SERVE
a bunch of fresh watercress
2 tablespoons olive oil
freshly squeezed juice of 1 lemon

a baking sheet lined with clingfilm/plastic wrap

MAKES 12 CAKES FOR 6 PEOPLE

Put the whole potatoes with the skin on in a large pot filled with water set over a medium–high heat. Boil for 15–20 minutes, or until cooked through. Drain and transfer to a plate to cool. Cover and chill in the fridge for at least 2 hours, or preferably overnight. This process of boiling the potatoes whole and refrigerating them removes a lot of their moisture which prevents the fishcakes from falling apart.

To prepare the haddock, place the milk and bay leaf in a large frying pan/skillet set over a medium heat and bring to the boil. Add the haddock, skin-side down. Reduce the heat and simmer for 3 minutes. Flip the fillets over, turn off the heat and allow the haddock to continue to cook in the residual heat.

Grate the chilled potatoes into a large mixing bowl – the skin should come away from the potato as you grate. Discard the skin and add the chopped herbs, melted butter, salt, pepper and beaten egg. Mix well.

Lift the haddock out of the milk, remove the skin and discard along with the milk. Flake the fish into chunks and add to the potato mixture. Stir gently to combine, taking care not to break up the fish pieces too much.

Form 12 round patties with your hands, of about 90 g/3 oz. each. Place the fishcakes on the prepared baking sheet, cover with clingfilm/plastic wrap and set in the fridge for at least 1 hour to firm up.

When ready to serve, preheat the oven to 160°C (325°F) Gas 3 and put a large saucepan or pot of water with a pinch of salt over a medium heat for poaching the eggs.

Heat 2 tablespoons of oil in a non-stick frying pan/skillet. Fry the fishcakes in batches for 3–4 minutes each side until lightly golden. Transfer to a baking sheet and keep warm in the oven while you cook the remaining fishcakes in the same way, adding more oil to the pan each time.

To poach the eggs, maintain the water at a gentle simmer. Crack an egg into a cup or ramekin and gently tip it into the pot. Repeat with the other eggs and cook for 4 minutes. Drain on a clean kitchen cloth or paper towels.

Mix all of the ingredients for the Dill Mayo together and season to taste with salt and pepper.

Serve the fishcakes with a poached egg on top, the Dill Mayo and some fresh watercress dressed with a little olive oil and lemon juice.

Bubble and squeak is a classic breakfast invention that transforms left over roast vegetables for the ultimate fry up.

PEAR & APPLE CHUTNEY

100 ml/⅓ cup
  vegetable oil
230 g/1½ cups (about 2
  small) finely diced
  red onion
1 kg/10 cups (about 7)
  finely diced apples
1 kg/4 cups (about 7)
  finely diced pears
250 g/1¼ cups soft
  brown sugar
250 g/1¼ cups dark
  brown sugar

200 ml/¾ cup red wine
  vinegar
10 g/2 tablespoons
  ground ginger
5 g/1 tablespoon
  ground coriander
5 g/1 tablespoon
  ground allspice

sterilized, glass jars
  with airtight lids

MAKES 1½ LITRES
(54 OZ.)/6 CUPS

Heat the oil in heavy-bottomed saucepan or pot set over a gentle heat. Sauté the onion, apples and pears until the onions are translucent. Add the remaining ingredients and simmer gently until the fruit is soft and the liquid has evaporated.

While still warm, spoon the chutney into sterilized, glass jars and, if not using straight away, seal and store following the instructions on page 17.

BUBBLE & SQUEAK

30 g/2 tablespoons
  unsalted butter
150 g/1 cup (about 1
  medium) sliced onion
1 garlic clove, finely
  chopped
220 g/3½ cups
  (about ¼) shredded
  white cabbage
400 g/2 cups mashed
  potato

500 g/2½ cups roast
  vegetables (squash,
  carrot and parsnip)
15 g/¼ cup flat-leaf
  parsley, chopped
sea salt and freshly
  ground black pepper
black pudding, thickly
  sliced and grilled
4 fried eggs
Pear & Apple Chutney
  (see opposite)

SERVES 4

Melt the butter in a non-stick frying pan/skillet set over a low–medium heat. Add the onion and garlic and cook for about 10 minutes, until soft and caramelised. Add the shredded cabbage and sweat down for 2–3 minutes. Add the mashed potato, other roast vegetables, parsley, salt and pepper, and mix well. Cook for a further 15–20 minutes, turning the vegetables from time to time and using a spatula to flatten the vegetables onto the base of the pan so that they catch and get a crispy bottom.

Serve with a fried egg, thick slices of grilled black pudding and some Pear & Apple Chutney.

You need to start this recipe a day in advance – the beans need to soak overnight and the ham hock can take up to 5 hours to cook. It's worth the wait though and Cheddar Cornbread (page 29) is the ideal accompaniment.

SLOW-BRAISED BEANS WITH HAM HOCK

500 g/1½ cups dried cannellini beans, soaked overnight
1½ teaspoons fennel seeds
1 x 2-kg/4½-lbs. ham hock
1 red (bell) pepper
2 tablespoons olive oil
1 onion, finely diced
2 garlic cloves, finely grated
2 x 400-g/14-oz. cans chopped tomatoes
1½ teaspoons dried chilli/chile flakes
1½ teaspoons sweet smoked paprika
500 ml/2 cups vegetable stock
75 ml/¼ cup black treacle/molasses
50 g/3 tablespoons tomato purée
500 ml/2 cups Worcestershire sauce
2 bay leaves
1 star anise
1½ teaspoons English mustard powder
a sprig of rosemary, roughly chopped
sea salt and freshly ground black pepper

a baking sheet lined with foil

SERVES 6–8

Soak the dried cannellini beans in water overnight, then rinse and discard the water.

Place the soaked beans, fennel seeds and ham hock in a large saucepan or pot and cover with cold water. Set over a medium–high heat and bring to the boil. Reduce the heat and simmer gently for about 45 minutes, until just soft. Drain, discard the water and reserve the beans, seeds and ham hock. Cover and set aside.

Preheat the oven to 200°C (400°F) Gas 6.

Place the pepper on the prepared baking sheet and place in the preheated oven for 20 minutes. Turn and roast for another 20 minutes, until the skin is blackened in most parts and the pepper collapses. Remove from oven and reduce the heat to 140°C (275°F) Gas 1. Put the pepper in a bowl, cover with clingfilm/plastic wrap and set aside for 10 minutes. Once the pepper is cool enough to handle, remove the skin, core and seeds, then dice the flesh.

Heat the olive oil in a frying pan/skillet set over a medium heat and sweat the onion until soft. Add the garlic and continue to cook for 1 minute before transferring to a

large, shallow, ovenproof casserole dish. Add the drained, cooked beans and seeds, the chopped tomatoes, peeled, roasted pepper, dried chilli/chile flakes, paprika, vegetable stock, black treacle, tomato purée, Worcestershire sauce, bay leaves, star anise, mustard powder and rosemary. Gently mix together.

Nestle the ham hock into the beans, cover with foil and cook in the still-warm oven for 3 hours. After this time, remove the foil and cook for another 1–2 hours, until the ham hock is cooked – the meat is cooked when it is easy to pull away from the bone.

Remove the dish from the oven and transfer the ham hock to a large plate to cool slightly. When it is cool enough to handle, cut off the skin and fat and discard. Shred the meat then return it to the casserole dish with the beans. Stir well, season with salt and pepper and serve.

VARIATION
For a vegetarian version of these slow-braised beans, omit the ham hock and reduce the final cooking stage, after you have removed the foil and returned the casserole dish to the oven, to 30 minutes.

Like the Courgette Loaf on page 39, this is more of a savoury cake than bread. Cut it into thick slices, butter each side and grill in a frying pan/skillet to get it nice and golden brown. Spread with Tomato Chilli Jam for a sweet and spicy kick.

TOMATO CHILLI JAM

1½ kg/8 cups ripe tomatoes

6 garlic cloves, finely grated

6 red chillies/chiles, deseeded and finely chopped

400 ml/1⅔ cups red wine vinegar

400 g/2 cups caster/granulated sugar

sterilized, glass jars with airtight lids

MAKES 1 LITRE (36 OZ.)/4 CUPS

To peel the tomatoes, cut a cross in the base of each tomato and place in a large mixing bowl. Cover with boiling water and set aside for 5 minutes. The skin should then peel away easily. Discard the skin, roughly chop the flesh of the tomatoes and place in a medium saucepan or pot set over a medium heat.

Add the remaining ingredients to the pan and bring to the boil, then reduce the heat and simmer for about 35 minutes, stirring occasionally, until thick and glossy.

Remove the pan from the heat, and while still warm, spoon the jam into sterilized, glass jars. Carefully tap them on the counter to get rid of any air pockets, wipe clean and tightly screw on the lids. Turn the jars upside down and leave until completely cold. Store unopened in a cool, dark place for up to 6 months or in the fridge for up to 2 months. Once opened, store in the fridge and use within 2 weeks.

CHEDDAR CORNBREAD

75 g/5 tablespoons melted butter, plus extra for greasing

250 ml/1 cup buttermilk

170 ml/⅔ cup milk

1 egg, lightly beaten

170 g/1⅓ cups cornmeal or quick-cook polenta

120 g/1¼ cups grated strong/sharp Cheddar cheese

3 Bird's eye chillies/chiles, deseeded and finely chopped

10 g/2 teaspoons salt

2 tablespoons chopped fresh chives

250 g/2 cups plain/all-purpose flour, sifted

10 g/2½ teaspoons baking powder

Tomato Chilli Jam, to serve (see opposite)

butter, to serve

a 900-g/2-lb loaf pan, greased and lined with baking parchment

MAKES 8 SLICES AND SERVES 4

Preheat the oven to 180°C (350°F) Gas 4.

Put the melted butter, buttermilk, milk, beaten egg and cornmeal in a large mixing bowl and set aside for 10 minutes.

Fold in the grated Cheddar, Bird's eye chillies/chiles, salt and chopped chives.

Sift in the flour and baking powder and fold until just combined, taking care not to over mix.

Pour into the prepared loaf pan and bake in the preheated oven for 30–35 minutes, until golden brown and a skewer comes out clean.

Set aside to cool in the pan for 5 minutes then turn out onto a wire rack to cool completely.

Slice, toast and butter the cornbread, and serve with Tomato Chilli Jam.

BEST BRUNCH EVER

'Brunch is cheerful, sociable and inciting. It is talk-compelling. It puts you in a good temper, it makes you satisfied with yourself and your fellow beings, it sweeps away the worries and cobwebs of the week.'
GUY BERINGER, 'BRUNCH: A PLEA', 1895.

I came to London on an ambitious mission: to convince the British that there are better ways to start the day than their most significant export, 'The Full English'. Even though our mothers told us that the first meal of the day is the most important, it is the meal that has historically been treated with the least respect, particularly in England. When in a fragile state, it might be a fry-up involving canned beans and fried eggs. When in a hurry, it's a bowl of cold, packet cereal or a processed muffin eaten with a milky, burnt coffee from a coffee chain store on the way to work. Worst of all, it gets missed altogether. As our first meal, it sets the tone for the rest of the day and should be given the care and attention it deserves.

Australia has developed a breakfast and brunch culture which rivals that of New York. It is an extremely social affair and the food is determinably inventive and multicultural. During the week, and always on the weekend, cafés are full of groups of friends sitting down to dishes as varied as miso porridge, a scrambled egg burrito, French toast with labne and orange blossom syrup or toasted pide with avocado.

Our Lantana cafés in London are open all day, but it is brunch that is our busiest and most popular service. Even though my aim was to convert the Brits to brunch culture, it still surprises me to see people queuing for a table at any café at 9 am. The most unassuming cafés, tucked down a side street, can quickly become places with queues around the block when tweeters and bloggers start spreading the word. Less surprising is the fact that it's the 20- and 30-somethings who have really answered the call to brunch. A lazy Sunday morning with friends is the perfect way to dissect the gossip from the night before, nurse sore heads with a 'hair of the dog' Bloody Mary and refill empty stomachs with plates of comforting sweet and savoury food.

The growing popularity of brunch also reflects the fact that cafés and restaurants now take this meal seriously. Gone are the days when you'd go out for breakfast and the extent of your choices would be eggs; scrambled, poached or fried. It's not uncommon to find cafés going the extra mile to make their own slow-braised baked beans or smoke their own salmon. And they're rewarded for their efforts when appreciative customers photograph their meal to share with the world. #bestbrunchever

This dish is inspired by the mushroom stall on Broadway market in London where they make amazing fried mushroom sandwiches for queues of hungry customers every Saturday. If a stall holder can pump out sandwiches this good using a single frying pan/skillet in the outdoors come wind, rain or snow, it seems the perfect quick dish for a small, busy café. Buttery mushrooms are a natural choice for breakfast, but they are also delicious stirred through pasta for an easy mid-week meal when you are low on time and energy.

SAUTÉED MIXED MUSHROOMS WITH LEMON HERBED FETA ON TOASTED SOURDOUGH

60 g/½ cup feta
¼ teaspoon grated lemon zest
1 tablespoon flat-leaf parsley, roughly chopped
2 sprigs of thyme, roughly chopped
2 teaspoons olive oil, plus 1 tablespoon for frying
30 g/2 tablespoons butter

400 g/6 cups mixed mushrooms (chesnut, flat, button, oyster), thickly sliced
1 garlic clove, crushed
sea salt and freshly ground black pepper
60 g/generous 1 cup spinach
4 slices sourdough bread

SERVES 2

Begin by making the herbed feta. Crumble the feta into a small mixing bowl. Add the lemon zest, parsley, thyme and 2 teaspoons of olive oil. Mash gently with a fork to combine and set aside.

To sauté the mushrooms, melt the butter and remaining 1 tablespoon of olive oil in a frying pan/skillet set over a high heat. Get the pan really hot without burning the butter before adding the mushrooms and garlic. Toss in the pan for a few minutes to coat the mushrooms, until they start to brown and crisp at the edges. Add a couple of good pinches of salt and freshly ground black pepper and allow the liquid in the mushrooms to evaporate, tossing the pan from time to time.

Add the spinach, stir through and remove the pan from the heat as it just starts to wilt. It will continue to cook from the heat of the mushrooms.

Toast the bread and pile each slice generously with the mushrooms and spinach. Crumble the herbed feta on top and serve.

There are many versions of this Middle Eastern dish on breakfast menus in cafés throughout Australia. I like plenty of sauce, which helps to cook the eggs and provides lots of juice to mop up with toast.

BAKED EGGS WITH CHORIZO, MUSHROOMS & LEMON CRÈME FRAÎCHE

4 eggs
sea salt and freshly ground black pepper, to season
Turkish bread, to serve

CHORIZO SAUCE
1 tablespoon olive oil
1 small red onion, finely chopped
2 garlic cloves, finely sliced
120 g/1 cup chorizo sausage, cut into ½-cm/¼-inch slices
1 x 400-g/14-oz. can plum tomatoes
1 tablespoon balsamic vinegar
1½ teaspoons soft brown sugar
¼ teaspoon chilli/chile flakes
½ star anise
1 x 5-cm/2-inch strip orange rind, pith removed
12 basil leaves, roughly torn

BAKED MUSHROOMS
15 g/1 tablespoon butter, plus extra for greasing
1 tablespoon olive oil
1 garlic clove, finely sliced
4 Portobello mushrooms, sliced

LEMON CRÈME FRAÎCHE
½ cup crème fraîche or sour/soured cream
¼ teaspoon grated lemon zest
½ teaspoon freshly squeezed lemon juice

a baking sheet, greased

SERVES 4

Begin by preparing the Chorizo Sauce. Put the oil in a large heavy-bottomed frying pan/skillet set over a low–medium heat and gently sauté the chopped onion for 7–10 minutes until soft and translucent, but not coloured. Add the sliced garlic and chorizo, and cook until the chorizo starts to brown and release its oils. Add 60 ml/¼ cup of water and all the remaining ingredients except the basil. Season with salt and pepper, turn up the heat and bring the mixture to the boil. Immediately reduce the heat and simmer for 20–30 minutes, until the sauce is thick and glossy. Remove from the heat, discard the star anise and orange rind, stir in the basil and set aside.

Preheat the oven to 180°C (350°F) Gas 4.

To prepare the mushrooms, melt the butter and olive oil in a frying pan/skillet set over a medium heat. Add the sliced garlic and allow it to cook gently for 2–3 minutes, then remove the pan from the heat. Place the mushrooms on the prepared baking sheet and spoon over the garlic-infused butter. Cover with foil and bake in the preheated oven for 15–20 minutes until tender.

To make the Lemon Crème Fraîche, combine all of the ingredients in a small mixing bowl, cover and set aside.

Return the Chorizo Sauce to a low heat and gently reheat. Add the Baked Mushrooms to the pan, making sure they are evenly distributed and half submerged in the sauce. Make four holes in the sauce with a wooden spoon and crack in the eggs. Cover and cook very gently for 15–20 minutes until the whites are set and the yolks still a little runny. Sprinkle with black pepper and serve with Turkish bread and Lemon Crème Fraîche.

Nothing says 'Saturday morning' better than French toast. The orange mascarpone cuts perfectly through the thick, eggy brioche and you can flavour the figs with your favourite honey – rose, vanilla and ginger all work well.

FRENCH TOAST WITH HONEY ROAST FIGS, ORANGE MASCARPONE & TOASTED ALMONDS

125 ml/½ cup mascarpone

2 tablespoons single/ light cream

½ teaspoon grated orange zest, plus extra to serve

1 tablespoon freshly squeezed orange juice

4 ripe figs, cut in half lengthways

clear honey, to drizzle

100 g/3½ oz. whole almonds

2 eggs

100 ml/½ cup milk

¼ teaspoon pure vanilla extract

1 tablespoons caster/ granulated sugar

2–4 thick slices of brioche

unsalted butter, for frying

icing/confectioners' sugar, for dusting

2 baking sheets, greased and lined with baking parchment

SERVES 2

Preheat the oven to 180°C (350°F) Gas 4.

Mix the mascarpone with the cream, orange zest and juice in a small mixing bowl. Cover and set aside or in the fridge until you are ready to serve.

Place the figs, cut-side up, on one of the prepared baking sheets. Drizzle with honey and roast in the preheated oven for 15–20 minutes until soft and caramelized. Remove from the oven and set aside until you are ready to serve.

Meanwhile, scatter the almonds on the other baking sheet and bake in the same oven for 8–10 minutes until lightly golden. Remove from the oven, cool completely then roughly chop.

To make the French toast, whisk together the eggs with the milk in a large mixing bowl. Add the vanilla and caster/granulated sugar, and whisk again. Transfer to a shallow dish and set aside.

Melt a little butter in a large frying pan/skillet set over a medium heat.

Dip each slice of brioche in the egg mixture one at a time. Let the slices soak up the egg mixture for a few seconds, then turn over to coat the other side.

Place the egg-soaked brioche slices in the hot pan and cook until golden on the bottom. Turn over and cook for a few minutes longer until each side is golden. Transfer to a clean baking sheet and put in the still-warm oven to keep warm while you cook the remaining slices. Cook the remaining toasts in the same way, adding a little more butter to the pan each time, if required.

To serve, cut the brioche in half diagonally. Overlap the triangles on the plate and top with the honey roast figs, orange mascarpone and toasted almonds. Sprinkle with a little extra orange zest and dust with icing/confectioners' sugar.

This is a great alternative to savoury muffins in the morning. Its loaf shape makes it easy to toast – thick slices, lightly toasted under a grill/broiler then spread with butter and Tomato Chilli Jam (page 29) beat savoury muffins hands down.

COURGETTE LOAF

300 g/4 cups (about 2) grated courgette/zucchini

300 g/2⅔ cups self-raising/rising flour, sifted

1 teaspoon baking powder

1 teaspoon mustard powder

½ teaspoon sea salt

½ teaspoon cayenne pepper

170 g/1⅔ cups grated strong/sharp Cheddar

100 g/6½ tablespoons butter, melted

4 eggs, beaten

135 ml/½ cup plus 1 tablespoon milk

a 900-g/2-lb loaf pan, greased and lined with baking parchment

MAKES 8 SLICES AND SERVES 4

Preheat the oven to 180°C (350°F) Gas 4.

Squeeze the grated courgette/zucchini with your hands to get rid of as much moisture as possible and place in a large mixing bowl with the flour, baking powder, mustard powder, salt, cayenne pepper and grated Cheddar. Toss everything together gently with your hands.

Combine the melted butter with the beaten eggs and milk in a jug/pitcher. Pour over the courgette/zucchini mixture and gently combine using a large spoon. Take care not to overwork the mixture – you should have a thick batter.

Spoon the mixture into the prepared loaf pan and bake in the preheated oven for 50 minutes– 1 hour, until golden brown and a skewer inserted into the middle comes out clean.

Set aside to cool in the pan for 5 minutes then turn out onto a wire rack to cool completely.

Slice, toast and butter the cornbread to serve.

This punchy little chutney with plenty of kick makes an excellent accompaniment to a sausage sandwich or strong Cheddar cheese and crackers.

PLUM CHUTNEY

1 kg/6 cups (about 40) roughly chopped firm ripe plums

1 kg/10 cups (about 7) peeled and roughly chopped cooking apples

5 garlic cloves, chopped

300 g/2 cups (about 2) finely diced onions

475 ml/scant 2 cups cider vinegar

150 g/1 cup (dark) raisins

8 whole cloves

2½ teaspoons chilli powder

2 large red chillies/ chiles, finely diced

½ cup freshly squeezed lemon juice

25 g/½ tablespoon ground cumin

420 g/2 cups plus 1 tablespoon soft brown sugar

2 teaspoons sea salt

1 cinnamon stick, broken in half

2½ teaspoons grated fresh ginger

sterilized, glass jars with airtight lids

MAKES 1½ LITRES (54 OZ.)/6 CUPS

Place the plums, apples, garlic and onions in a saucepan or pot set over a gentle heat and slowly bring to the boil. Reduce the heat and simmer for 20–25 minutes, stirring occasionally.

Place the remaining ingredients in a large mixing bowl and stir well. Pour into the simmering plum mixture and stir using a wooden spoon. Continue to simmer for 1–1¼ hours, stirring occasionally, until the mixture is thick and glossy.

Remove the pan from the heat, discard the cinnamon and while still warm, spoon the chutney into sterilized, glass jars. Carefully tap them on the counter to get rid of any air pockets, wipe clean and tightly screw on the lids. Turn the jars upside down and leave until completely cold. Store unopened in a cool, dark place for up to 6 months or in the fridge for up to 2 months. Once opened, store in the fridge and use within 2 weeks.

Corn fritters are a menu staple in nearly every café in Australia and New Zealand. No two recipes are ever the same as everyone has their (strong!) opinion on what makes the perfect fritter.

CORN FRITTERS WITH ROAST TOMATOES & SMASHED AVOCADOS

150 g/2 cups (about 1 medium) grated courgette/zucchini
sea salt and freshly ground black pepper, to season
400 g/2½ cups cherry vine tomatoes
olive oil, to drizzle
4 eggs
180 g/1⅓ cups self-raising/rising flour
50 g/1¾ oz. Parmesan, grated
100 ml/scant ½ cup buttermilk
1 teaspoon paprika
½ teaspoon cayenne pepper
1 tablespoon chopped coriander/cilantro
fresh corn kernels cut from 2–3 cobs
sunflower oil, for frying

SMASHED AVOCADOS
3 avocados
freshly squeezed juice of 2 limes and the grated zest of 1
¼ red onion, finely diced
1 teaspoon hot sauce

TO SERVE
fresh spinach
crème fraîche

SERVES 6

Put the grated courgette/zucchini into a colander set over a large mixing bowl. Sprinkle with ½ teaspoon of salt and leave for 30 minutes–1 hour so they release their moisture. Squeeze the grated courgette/zucchini with your hands to get rid of as much moisture as possible and set aside.

For the roast tomatoes, preheat the oven to 180°C (350°F) Gas 4. Place the tomatoes on a baking sheet, drizzle with olive oil and season with salt and pepper. Roast in the preheated oven for 15–20 minutes, or until the skins begin to split.

Reduce the oven temperature to 170°C (325°F) Gas 3 and prepare the fritter batter. In a large, clean, dry mixing bowl, lightly whisk the eggs. Add in the flour, grated Parmesan, buttermilk, paprika, cayenne pepper, ½ teaspoon of salt, a pinch of pepper and chopped coriander/cilantro. Stir in the squeezed courgette/zucchini and corn kernels, ensuring the vegetables are evenly coated in batter.

Add enough sunflower oil to thinly cover the bottom of a heavy-bottomed frying pan/skillet. Ladle generous spoonfuls of batter into the pan and cook for about 4 minutes on each side, until golden brown. Transfer to a clean baking sheet and put in the still-warm oven for 4–5 minutes to ensure they are cooked through. Cook the remaining batter in the same way, adding a little more oil to the pan each time, if required.

Just before serving, roughly mash the avocados with a fork, leaving them fairly chunky. Stir in the lime juice and zest, onion and hot sauce. Season generously with salt and serve with the fritters, roast tomatoes, a handful of fresh spinach and a dollop of crème fraîche.

It is virtually impossible to make an espresso coffee at home that is as good as one made in a café by a trained barista using expensive commercial machinery. But if you want a hassle-free, inexpensive method for making delicious coffee at home, my advice is to make a filter coffee instead. Filter coffee is a longer, less intense drink than an espresso. By pouring the water slowly over coffee by hand, you can extract more of the delicate flavours and get to taste the characteristics of the coffee. Lighter roasted, single origin coffee is ideal for this method of coffee brewing.

POUR-OVER COFFEE

17–18 g/¼ cup coffee beans
250–280 ml/1–1¼ cups boiling water

EQUIPMENT
a coffee grinder
a single-cup drip coffee
   cone and filter paper
a watch or timer
weighing scales
a pouring kettle or
   jug/pitcher (optional)

SERVES 1

It's always best to use freshly ground coffee so it is worth investing in a small domestic grinder for home. Hand grinders are perfect if you are just making one or two cups. Grind your coffee beans on a medium grind for a paper filter.

Next, measure out your boiled water. You don't want to use the water as soon as it boils as this will burn the coffee. Pour 250 ml/1 cup into a pouring kettle or jug/pitcher while you're getting everything else ready, as this will allow the temperature to drop slightly.

Line your single-cup drip coffee cone with the paper filter and rinse it with hot water from the tap. This helps to get rid of the paper taste and allows the coffee to filter through more easily.

Put the ground coffee in the moistened filter and place it on top of your cup. Pour in enough boiled and slightly cooled water from your pouring kettle to saturate the grinds – the coffee will bloom and bubble. Over the next 3 minutes, very slowly pour the remaining water over the coffee. Pour in a circular motion to get an even distribution.

After 3 minutes you should have used up nearly all of the water in your pouring kettle, the water will have filtered through the ground coffee and your Pour-over Coffee is ready!

BEST EVER BLOODY MARY

500 ml/2 cups tomato
    juice
1 x Roast Tomatoes
    (see page 43)
30 ml/2 tablespoons
    Worcestershire sauce
30 ml/2 tablespoons
    Sriracha Chilli sauce
a 3-cm/1¼-inch piece
    of horseradish, finely
    grated

sea salt and freshly
    ground black pepper
60 ml/¼ cup freshly
    squeezed lime juice
300 ml/1¼ cups vodka

TO GARNISH
Pickled Celery
    (see below)
chilli/chile flakes

SERVES 4

Put the tomato juice and Roast Tomatoes
in a food processor and blend until smooth.

Transfer to a jug/pitcher and stir in the
Worcestershire sauce, Sriracha chilli sauce and
grated horseradish. Season with salt and pepper,
cover with clingfilm/plastic wrap and chill in the
fridge for at least 30 minutes.

When ready to serve, add the lime juice and
vodka, and stir well. Place a pickled celery stick
in 6 high-ball glasses, fill each glass with ice and
pour in the Bloody Mary mixture. Garnish each
with a pinch of chilli/chile flakes and enjoy!

PICKLED CELERY

1 head celery, peeled
    and trimmed to
    sticks taller than
    your serving glass
500 g/2½ cups caster/
    granulated sugar
1 litre/4 cups white
    wine vinegar
2 tablespoons sea salt
8 garlic cloves, chopped
2 teaspoons mustard

seeds
2 teaspoons chilli/hot
    red pepper flakes
2 teaspoons black
    peppercorns

sterilized, glass jars
    with airtight lids

MAKES 500 ML
(18 OZ.)/2 CUPS

Stand the celery sticks in a tall, sterilized,
glass jar. Place the remaining ingredients in
a saucepan or pot with 250 ml/1 cup of water. Set
over a medium–high heat and bring to the boil.
Continue to boil for 15 minutes, remove
from the heat and cover to stop the liquor
evaporating. Set aside to cool slightly, then pour
into the jar with the celery sticks. Wipe the jar
clean and tightly screw on the lid. Turn upside
down and leave until completely cold. The celery
is best made a day or two in advance.

A Bloody Mary is the ultimate brunch drink, allowing you to ingest booze before midday with complete legitimacy and even a hint of old-fashioned sophistication. Roast Tomatoes add a deep and rich flavour and Pickled Celery gives a tangy zing but you can substitute these for fresh tomatoes and raw celery if you're short of time.

These spiced lamb skewers are more sophisticated than your average late night kebab/kabob, but just as tempting. Keep them nice and juicy by not overcooking the lamb.

LAMB KOFTES WITH TAHINI YOGURT DIP

1 kg/3 lbs. minced/ ground lamb

1½ teaspoons ground cumin

1½ teaspoons smoked sweet paprika

1 teaspoon ground allspice

1 teaspoon chilli powder

150 g/1 cup (about 1 medium) finely diced red onion

25 g/½ cup flat-leaf parsley, finely chopped

40 g/¾ cup coriander/ cilantro, finely chopped, plus extra to serve

freshly squeezed juice and grated zest of 1 lemon, plus wedges to serve

3 large eggs

1 teaspoon sea salt

60 ml/¼ cup sunflower oil, for frying

TAHINI YOGURT DIP

250 ml/1 cup Greek yogurt

25 ml/2 tablespoons tahini paste

2 tablespoons freshly squeezed lemon juice

10 g/¼ cup mint, finely chopped

¼ cucumber, grated

1 garlic clove, crushed

½ teaspoon sea salt

TO SERVE

coriander/cilantro, roughly chopped

lemon wedges

30 x 15-cm/6-inch wooden skewers, soaked in water for at least 30 minutes

MAKES 30 SKEWERS AND SERVES 10–15

To make the koftes, place all of the ingredients except the oil in a large mixing bowl and mix everything together using your hands.

Shape the kofte mixture around the soaked skewers (about 45–50 g/1½–2 oz. per skewer) in a sausage shape and press the mince firmly together. Transfer to a baking sheet, cover with clingfilm/plastic wrap and set in the fridge for at least 2 hours, or preferably overnight, to firm up.

Preheat the oven to 180°C (350°F) Gas 4.

Heat the sunflower oil in a large frying pan/ skillet set over a medium–high heat. Add the koftes in batches and cook for about 4 minutes, turning them until golden brown all over. Transfer to a clean baking sheet, while you cook the remaining koftes in the same way, adding more oil to the pan each time if necessary.

When all the koftes have been fried, place them in the preheated oven for 5 minutes to cook through.

To make the Tahini Yogurt Dip, mix all the ingredients together and season with sea salt to taste.

Serve the koftes on a platter scattered with chopped coriander/cilantro, with lemon wedges and the tahini yogurt dip on the side.

The good news is, you don't need a deep fryer to make salt and pepper squid at home. A frying pan/skillet or wok does the job. The bad news is these delicious crispy squid taste so good because they're cooked in lots of oil. But get the oil hot enough and these squid morsels will be surprisingly light and not at all greasy or heavy.

SALT & PEPPER SQUID WITH LIME AIOLI

600 g/1¼ lbs. squid, cleaned
75 g/½ cup rice flour or cornflour/cornstarch
1 teaspoon Chinese five spice
1 teaspoon sea salt
1 teaspoon freshly ground white or black pepper
vegetable oil, for frying
1 long red chilli/chile, deseeded and thinly sliced
20 g/scant ½ cup coriander/cilantro
wedges of lime, to garnish

LIME AIOLI
2 egg yolks
1 garlic clove, crushed
2 teaspoons Dijon mustard
250 ml/1 cup olive oil
freshly squeezed juice and grated zest of 1 lime
sea salt and freshly ground black pepper, to season

SERVES 4–6

Begin by preparing the Lime Aioli. Place the egg yolks, garlic and mustard in a food processor and blitz to a paste. With the motor still running very slowly add the oil in a slow, steady drizzle until it forms a thick sauce. Stir in the lime juice, zest and 2 tablespoons of water. Season with salt and pepper to taste, then cover and set in the fridge until you are ready to serve.

To prepare the squid, cut down the 'seam' of the squid so it opens out flat. Pat dry with paper towels. Score the inside with a cross-hatch pattern then slice the squid lengthways into 2-cm/¾-inch strips.

Mix the rice flour, Chinese five spice, salt and pepper together in a shallow dish or plate. Toss the squid pieces in the seasoned flour to coat.

Pour enough vegetable oil into a frying pan/skillet or wok so that it has a depth of about 2½ cm/1 inch. Set over a high heat and bring to a smoking heat. Test whether it is hot enough to fry the squid by flicking some flour into the oil – it should sizzle vigorously.

Shake off any excess flour from the squid strips and fry in the hot oil in batches for 2–3 minutes, until lightly golden brown.

Remove the squid from the oil with a slotted spoon and drain on paper towels, while you cook the remaining strips in the same way. When all the squid is cooked, transfer to a large mixing bowl. Add the sliced chilli/chile and chopped coriander/cilantro and toss the squid to coat.

Heap the squid onto a serving platter garnished with lime wedges and lime aioli on the side to dip into.

Pork. How do I love thee? Let me count the ways. Roasted, pulled, in a bun, slow cooked, and sweet and sour. Best of all I love it with spicy, crispy skin and bite-sized. Yes, it really is as good as it sounds and makes a fantastic appetizer or hand-around canapé. Don't be put off by all the steps as they are not difficult and this is one of those perfect party dishes that can be prepared days in advance and then grilled in minutes when ready to serve.

CRISPY PORK BELLY BITES

85 g/¼ cup clear honey
5 bay leaves
3 sprigs rosemary
250 g/1 cup sea salt
2 tablespoons peppercorns
a small bunch of fresh thyme
1 bulb of garlic, cloves removed and flattened with skin on
1½ kg/4½ lbs. pork belly, skin on
2 litres/8 cups olive oil

TO SERVE
Nahm Jim Dipping Sauce (see page 58)
coriander/cilantro, roughly chopped, to garnish

a baking sheet, greased and lined with baking parchment

SERVES 8–10

Begin by brining the pork. Combine the honey, bay leaves, rosemary, salt, peppercorns, thyme, garlic and 3 litres/12 cups of water in a container large enough to hold the pork.

Place the pork in the brine, cover and set in the fridge for at least 12 hours or overnight.

Remove the pork from the brine and discard the brine. Rinse the pork in a large bowl under running water, then pat dry with paper towels.

To confit the pork, preheat the oven to 120°C (250°F) Gas ½. Place the rinsed pork in a roasting pan and pour over the olive oil. Cover with foil and cook in the preheated oven for 4½ hours. The oil will gently bubble and poach the pork, until it is soft and falling apart.

Remove from the oven, uncover slightly and allow the pork to cool to room temperature.

Press the pork so that it has a nice, firm texture, by removing it from the oil and place it, rind-side down, on the prepared

baking sheet. Keep the oil to one side for crisping the skin later. Cover the pork with clingfilm/plastic wrap and weigh it down with something heavy like a big wooden chopping board or a cast-iron roasting dish. Set in the fridge for at least 12 hours.

When ready to serve, preheat the oven to 220°C (425°F) Gas 7.

Score the skin of the pressed pork with a diamond pattern and cut into 2-cm/¾-inch squares.

Drizzle a clean baking sheet with a little of the reserved cooking oil, place the pork squares skin-side down and roast for 15 minutes, until the skin is golden brown and crisp. Remove from the oven and drain on paper towels. Alternatively, you can crisp up the skin by placing the pork, skin-side up, underneath a grill/broiler on a medium heat for 3–4 minutes.

Transfer to a serving platter, garnish with coriander/cilantro and serve with Nahm Jim Dipping Sauce on the side.

Corn gives these canapés a slight twist on the traditional smoked salmon blinis. The blinis can be made ahead of time but assemble just before serving.

CORN FRITTER BLINIS WITH SMOKED SALMON & LEMON CREAM

225 g/2 cups (about 1 medium) grated courgette/zucchini
4 eggs
180 g/1⅓ cups self-raising/rising flour
50 g/1¾ oz. Parmesan, grated
100 ml/scant ½ cup buttermilk
1 teaspoon paprika
½ teaspoon cayenne pepper
1 tablespoon chopped coriander/cilantro
fresh corn kernels cut from 2–3 cobs
sunflower oil, for frying
sea salt and freshly ground black pepper, to season
300 g/1½ cups smoked salmon, to serve
chervil or chopped chives, to garnish

LEMON CREAM
250 ml/1 cup sour/soured cream
1 tablespoon freshly squeezed lemon juice
1 teaspoon grated lemon zest
¼ teaspoon sea salt

MAKES 30–35 AND SERVES 10–15

Put the grated courgette/zucchini into a colander set over a large mixing bowl. Sprinkle with ½ teaspoon of salt and leave for 30 minutes–1 hour so they release their moisture. Squeeze the grated courgette/zucchini with your hands to get rid of as much moisture as possible and set aside.

In a large, clean, dry mixing bowl, lightly whisk the eggs. Add the flour, grated Parmesan, buttermilk, paprika, cayenne pepper, ½ teaspoon of salt, black pepper and chopped coriander/cilantro. Stir in the squeezed courgette/zucchini and corn kernels, ensuring the vegetables are evenly coated in batter.

Add enough sunflower oil to thinly cover the bottom of a heavy-bottomed frying pan/skillet.

Drop small spoonfuls of batter into the pan using a teaspoon and cook for about 2 minutes on each side, until golden brown. Drain on paper towels, then transfer to a clean baking sheet. Cook the remaining batter in the same way, adding a little more oil to the pan each time, if required. If you are not going to assemble the blinis straight away, cool completely and cover with clingfilm/plastic wrap.

To make the Lemon Cream, combine the sour/soured cream, lemon juice and zest and salt in a small bowl.

Arrange the blinis on a serving platter, top with a ribbon of smoked salmon and a dollop of Lemon Cream. Garnish with chervil or chopped chives and a sprinkle of freshly ground black pepper.

I vividly remember the first time I tried fishcakes in a Thai restaurant with my parents when I was about 10 years old. A defining food moment. I tried to recreate those fishcakes with this recipe and packed them full of fresh Asian flavours. It is one of our most popular dishes at the café.

THAI FISHCAKES WITH NAHM JIM DIPPING SAUCE

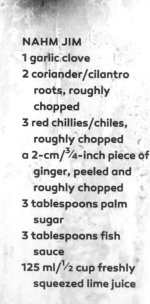

NAHM JIM
1 garlic clove
2 coriander/cilantro roots, roughly chopped
3 red chillies/chiles, roughly chopped
a 2-cm/¾-inch piece of ginger, peeled and roughly chopped
3 tablespoons palm sugar
3 tablespoons fish sauce
125 ml/½ cup freshly squeezed lime juice

FISHCAKES
500 g/1¼ lbs. haddock or other white fish, roughly chopped
2 red chillies/chiles, roughly chopped
3 spring onions/ scallions, roughly chopped
5 lime leaves, chopped
2 garlic cloves, roughly chopped
a 2-cm/¾-inch piece of ginger, peeled and roughly chopped
1 tablespoon fish sauce
200 g/¾ cup prawns/ shrimp, peeled and roughly chopped
50 g/1 cup coriander/ cilantro, finely chopped plus extra to serve
vegetable oil, for frying

2 baking sheets, 1 greased and lined with baking parchment

MAKES 12 AND SERVES 4

Put 100 g/3½ oz. of the fish, the chillies/chiles, spring onions/scallions, lime leaves, garlic, ginger, and fish sauce in a large mixing bowl and stir well to combine. Blitz to a paste consistency using a handheld electric mixer or in a food processor. This paste is used to bind the fishcakes.

Mix the paste with the remaining fish, prawns/ shrimp and coriander/cilantro. Form 12 round patties with your hands, of about 75 g/3 oz. each. Place the fishcakes on the unlined baking sheet, cover with clingfilm/plastic wrap and set in the fridge for at least 2 hours to firm up. As there is no egg to bind the mixture in this recipe, they do need time in the fridge to firm up. I find omitting egg gives the fishcakes a lighter texture.

When ready to serve, preheat the oven to 180°C (350°F) Gas 4 and cover the bottom of a non-stick frying pan/skillet with vegetable oil, about ½ cm/ inch deep. Sear the fishcakes in batches for 2 minutes on each side until lightly golden. Transfer to the lined baking sheet while you cook the remaining fishcakes in the same way. When all the fishcakes are seared, transfer to the preheated oven for another 3 minutes to cook through.

To make the Nahm Jim dipping sauce, pound the garlic, coriander/cilantro roots, chillies/chiles and ginger in a pestle and mortar to a rough paste. Add the palm sugar, fish sauce and lime juice and mix thoroughly. Add more palm sugar, lime or fish sauce if necessary to get the desired balance of sweet, sour and salty.

Serve the fishcakes with the Nahm Jim, dressed with fresh coriander/cilantro.

A frittata is a baked omelette that is delicious at anytime of the day, served hot or cold. We often make one for the breakfast counter at the café, cut into wedges for our takeaway customers but it also makes a great canapé – cut into small bite-sized squares which can be picked up with a toothpick.

CHORIZO, RED PEPPER & PEA FRITTATA BITES

4 x 60-g/2-oz. chorizo
    sausages
16 eggs
300 ml/1¼ cups crème
    fraîche
a pinch of salt and
    freshly ground black
    pepper
1 tablespoon olive oil
150 g/1 cup (about
    1 medium) finely
    chopped red onion
1 garlic clove, crushed
130 g/1 cup fresh or
    frozen peas
1 red (bell) pepper,
    deseeded and cut
    into strips
60 g/1¼ cups baby
    spinach

SERVES 8–10

Preheat the oven to 180°C (350°F) Gas 4.

Place the chorizo sausages on a baking sheet and cook in the preheated oven for 12 minutes. Remove from the oven, drain on paper towels and cut into 1-cm/⅜-inch slices. Cover and set aside.

Reduce the oven temperature to 110°C (225°F) Gas ¼.

Put the eggs in a large mixing bowl with the crème fraîche and lightly whisk to combine. Season with salt and pepper, and set aside.

Heat the oil in a large non-stick, ovenproof frying pan/skillet set over a low–medium heat. Add the onion and garlic and sauté, until soft but not coloured.

Add the sliced chorizo, peas and pepper strips and cook for 2–3 minutes, stirring occasionally.

Add the baby spinach and stir until the spinach just begins to wilt.

Arrange the mix evenly over the base of the pan and carefully pour in the egg mixture.

Reduce the heat and gently cook the frittata, moving the egg in a little from the edge of the pan as it cooks (similar to how you would cook an omelette) using a spatula to run around the outside of the pan. You don't want to get any colour on the base of the frittata so it is important to keep the temperature low.

Continue running the spatula around the outside of the pan to ensure the frittata doesn't stick.

After about 10 minutes, once it has just set on the bottom and the sides, place the pan in the oven for 15–20 minutes, until the frittata is lightly golden and just set in the middle. Remove from the oven and set aside to cool for 10 minutes.

Once cool, cover the pan with a chopping board and turn it over to release the frittata. Cut it into 4-cm/1½-inch squares and transfer to a plate to serve.

The secret to making these ribs meltingly tender is to braise them slowly before cooking them in the sticky marinade. I've made this recipe many times with both pork ribs as well as beef short ribs and really can't decide which I prefer. The pork ribs are easier for handing around to eat with fingers whereas the beef ribs are larger and better served with a knife and fork and some steamed rice. Whichever you go for, they are unbelievably good.

STICKY ASIAN RIBS

2 kg/6 lbs. meaty pork ribs or beef short ribs
125 ml/½ cup light soy sauce
60 ml/¼ cup dark soy sauce
250 ml/1 cup Chinese cooking wine
1 long red chilli/chile, sliced into rounds
4 x 5-cm/2-in pieces of ginger, sliced
4 garlic cloves, sliced
100 g/½ cup crushed yellow rock sugar
4 whole star anise
6 spring onions/scallions, trimmed

STICKY MARINADE
2 tablespoons dark soy sauce
6 garlic cloves, peeled and sliced
4 tablespoons clear honey
3 tablespoons hoisin sauce
½ teaspoon ground ginger
1 teaspoon Chinese five spice
1 tablespoon sesame oil

SERVES 6

Preheat the oven to 150°C (300°F) Gas 2.

Place the pork or beef ribs in a large baking dish bone-side up. Add the remaining ingredients and 750 ml/3 cups of water. Cover with foil and place in the preheated oven to braise for 3 hours.

Meanwhile, prepare the Sticky Marinade. Combine all of the marinade ingredients in a small mixing bowl, cover and set aside or in the fridge until ready to use.

Remove the ribs from the oven, lift out of the pan and discard the braising liquid. They should be really tender after braising and you can keep them in the fridge, ready to cook another time, at this point.

When ready to serve, preheat the oven to 200°C (400°F) Gas 6.

Cut the ribs into individual portions, place in an ovenproof baking dish and smother them with the sticky marinade.

Cook in the preheated oven for about 15 minutes, until bubbling and sticky, turning once halfway through cooking.

Pile the ribs high on a platter. Hand round some napkins – this can get messy.

Chutneys and preserves are the unsung heroes of the culinary world; always an accompaniment and never the star of the show. For me, they deserve centre stage. They lend themselves so beautifully to café food as they spice up the simplest of dishes – Kasoundi with melted cheese on toast, cornbread with chilli jam, or grilled black pudding with apple and pear compote. The beauty of making your own preserves is that you can make big batches at a time and fill your store cupboard with treasures that only improve with age.

KASOUNDI WITH CHEESE ON TOAST

5 x 5-cm/2-in piece of ginger, peeled and finely chopped

1 bulb garlic, chopped

30 g/¼ cup (about 2) deseeded and chopped green chillies/chiles

250 ml/1 cup malt vinegar

70 ml/¼ cup vegetable oil

45 g/4½ tablespoons black mustard seeds

15 g/2 tablespoons turmeric powder

45 g/5 tablespoons ground cumin

20 g/3 tablespoons chilli powder

1 kg/5 cups firm ripe tomatoes, chopped

30 g/6 teaspoons sea salt

125 g/½ cup soft brown sugar

sterilized, glass jars with airtight lids

MAKES 1½ LITRES (54 OZ.)/6 CUPS

Place the ginger, garlic and chillies/chiles with 25 ml/1½ tablespoons of the vinegar in a food processor and blend to a smooth paste.

Heat the oil in a heavy-bottomed saucepan or pot set over a medium heat. Add the mustard seeds, turmeric, cumin and chilli powder. Stir and cook for about 4 minutes, taking care not to let the mixture stick to the bottom of the pan, blacken or burn.

Pour in the ginger paste and cook for a further 5 minutes. Add the tomatoes, salt, remaining vinegar and sugar. Reduce the heat and simmer for 1–1½ hours, stirring occasionally to prevent sticking.

The Kasoundi is ready when it is thick and there is a trace of oil on top.

While still warm, spoon the Kasoundi into sterilized, glass jars. Carefully tap them on the counter to get rid of any air pockets, wipe clean and tightly screw on the lids. Turn the jars upside down and leave until completely cold.

Store unopened in a cool, dark place for up to 6 months. Once opened store in the fridge and use within 2 weeks.

Dukkha is an Egyptian dry spice blend that has a multitude of uses – as a salad sprinkle, a seasoning on lamb chops, or a dip with bread and olive oil. We serve it as a pre-dinner bar snack with hard-boiled eggs.

DUKKHA WITH HARD-BOILED EGGS

100 g/1 cup roasted and peeled hazelnuts
20 g/$\frac{1}{4}$ cup roasted pistachio nuts
15 g/2 tablespoons coriander seeds
1 tablespoon cumin seeds
40 g/5 tablespoons sesame seeds
2 teaspoons white or black peppercorns
$\frac{1}{2}$ teaspoon chilli/chile flakes
$\frac{1}{2}$ teaspoon sea salt
8–10 eggs, to serve

MAKES 350 ML
(12 OZ.)/1$\frac{1}{2}$ CUPS
AND SERVES 4

Preheat the oven to 170°C (325°F) Gas 3.

Place the hazelnuts and pistachio nuts on separate baking sheets and roast in the preheated oven for 10 minutes.

Remove from the oven and immediately wrap the hazelnuts in a clean kitchen towel. Set aside to allow the steam to build for a minute before rubbing them within the kitchen towel to remove the loose skins. When both the pistachio nuts and hazelnuts are cool, roughly crush them in a pestle and mortar to a chunky texture. Transfer the mixture to a large mixing bowl.

Place the coriander and cumin seeds in a preheated frying pan/skillet set over a medium heat. Dry fry the seeds for a couple of minutes, shaking the pan from time to time, until they start to pop. Remove the seeds from the pan and crush in a pestle and mortar. Add to the nuts in the mixing bowl.

Place the sesame seeds in the same, dry pan and toast until lightly golden, giving the pan a shake

every 30 seconds. Remove from the pan and grind in the pestle and mortar. Add to the nut and seed mixture.

Repeat this process with the white or black peppercorns.

Lightly grind the chilli/chile flakes in the pestle and mortar and add to the nut and seed mixture.

Finally, add the salt and mix everything together. The dukkha is now ready and can be stored in an airtight container for up to 2 weeks.

Place the eggs in a saucepan or pot with enough cold water to cover them by 2$\frac{1}{2}$ cm/1 inch. Set over a medium–high heat and bring the water to the boil. As soon as it reaches the boil, reduce the heat and simmer for 7 minutes. Remove the pan from the heat, discard the cooking water and rinse under cold, running water for 1 minute. Set aside to cool completely in the pan filled with cold water. This cooling method helps to prevent a dark ring forming between the yolk and the white.

Peel the eggs and dip the tops in the dukkha. They're delicious!

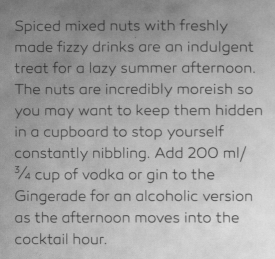

Spiced mixed nuts with freshly made fizzy drinks are an indulgent treat for a lazy summer afternoon. The nuts are incredibly moreish so you may want to keep them hidden in a cupboard to stop yourself constantly nibbling. Add 200 ml/ ¾ cup of vodka or gin to the Gingerade for an alcoholic version as the afternoon moves into the cocktail hour.

SPICED MIXED NUTS

500 g/5 cups assorted unsalted nuts (cashews, hazelnuts, brazil nuts, peanuts, blanched almonds, pecans, walnuts)

1 tablespoon fennel seeds

15 g/2 tablespoons sesame seeds

100 g/¾ cup pumpkin seeds

1½ tablespoons (about 2 sprigs) coarsely chopped rosemary

1 teaspoon chilli/chile flakes

4 teaspoons dark muscovado sugar

1 teaspoon sea salt

2 tablespoons melted unsalted butter

MAKES 950 ML
(32 OZ.)/4 CUPS

Preheat the oven to 180°C (350°F) Gas 4.

Mix the nuts together in a bowl and then spread on a baking sheet.

Toast in the preheated oven for about 10 minutes, until lightly golden brown. Keep a close eye on them though as the nuts can burn quickly.

Meanwhile, place the fennel, sesame and pumpkin seeds in a preheated frying pan/skillet set over a medium heat. Dry fry the seeds for a few minutes until the sesame seeds turn lightly golden brown.

Put the rosemary, chilli/chile flakes, sugar, salt and melted butter in a large mixing bowl and stir to combine.

While the nuts and seeds are still warm from the oven and pan, toss in the butter spice mixture to coat thoroughly.

HOMEMADE GINGERADE

200 g/1 cup demerara/
  turbinado sugar
40 g/4 tablespoons
  grated fresh ginger
freshly squeezed juice
  of 6–8 limes

a bunch of mint leaves,
  gently bruised
soda water, to top up
ice and sliced lime, to
  serve

SERVES 6

Place the sugar, grated ginger and 250 ml/1 cup water in a saucepan or pot set over a medium heat. Stir continuously until the sugar has dissolved. Bring to the boil, then immediately reduce the heat and simmer gently for 10 minutes. Remove the pan from the heat and set aside to cool for at least 1 hour. The longer it infuses the more gingery your syrup.

Add the lime juice and bruised mint leaves.

Half fill your serving jug or high-ball glasses with ice. Pour in the ginger–lime syrup (about 60 ml/¼ cup per person). Top with soda water and lime slices, and serve.

PINK FIZZ

200 g/1 cup caster/
  granulated sugar
1 tablespoon dried
  hibiscus flowers

Prosecco or champagne,
  to top up

SERVES 6

Place the sugar, 500 ml/2 cups of water and hibiscus flowers in a saucepan or pot set over a medium heat. Stir continuously until the sugar has dissolved. Bring to the boil, then remove the pan from the heat and allow the mixture to infuse for 20 minutes. Strain the syrup through a fine, mesh sieve/strainer set over a large mixing bowl, then set aside to cool.

Pour into an airtight bottle or container and chill in the fridge until ready to use.

Pour 15 ml/1 tablespoon of the hibiscus syrup into the base of each champagne flute. Top with prosecco or champagne and serve.

The syrup will keep in the fridge for 3 weeks and is delicious in many forms – as a cordial base for other drinks, poured over ice cream or frozen as an ice lolly.

Quinoa is one of those slightly tricky grains that can be bland and soggy if under-seasoned and overcooked. I find that toasting the quinoa before boiling it in water gives it a lovely nutty flavour and helps it retain its texture.

QUINOA & RED RICE SALAD WITH CASHEW NUTS & CITRUS GINGER DRESSING

2 medium red onions, peeled and cut into wedges, root intact
3 tablespoons olive oil
1 teaspoon brown sugar
sea salt and freshly ground black pepper, to season
60 g/$\frac{2}{3}$ cup cashew nuts
200 g/1$\frac{1}{4}$ cups quinoa
200 g/1 cup Camargue red rice
100 g/$\frac{2}{3}$ cup (dark) raisins

2 handfuls of rocket/arugula
4 spring onions/scallions, thinly sliced

DRESSING
5 tablespoons olive oil
1 tablespoon sesame oil
freshly squeezed juice and grated zest of 1 orange
1 tablespoon rice wine vinegar
a 5-cm/2-in piece of ginger, peeled and finely grated
1 long red chilli/chile, deseeded and finely diced
1 garlic clove, finely grated

SERVES 6

Preheat the oven to 170°C (325°F) Gas 3.

Put the onion wedges on a baking sheet and drizzle with the olive oil, sprinkle with brown sugar and season with salt and pepper. Roast in the preheated oven for 25 minutes, until meltingly soft. Remove from the oven and set aside to cool completely.

Meanwhile, scatter the cashew nuts on a separate baking sheet and toast in the same oven as the onion for 8 minutes. Remove from oven and set aside to cool.

Once you have roasted the cashew nuts, spread the quinoa evenly on another baking sheet and toast in the same oven for 10 minutes.

Set 2 saucepans or pots filled with salted water over a medium heat and bring to the boil. Add the red rice to one pan and simmer for 20 minutes. Add the toasted quinoa to the other pan and simmer for 9 minutes. Once cooked, both should still have a little bite.

Drain off the water in both pans using a fine, mesh sieve/strainer. Transfer the quinoa and rice to a large mixing bowl and set aside to cool.

To make the Citrus Ginger Dressing, mix all of the ingredients together in a small bowl, using a whisk to emulsify the oils with the orange juice and vinegar.

Pour the dressing into the bowl with the rice and quinoa. Add the roasted red onions, toasted cashew nuts, (dark) raisins, rocket/arugula, and spring onions/scallions. Season with salt and pepper and serve.

This is a salad of contrasts. Sweet and bitter, soft and crunchy, and a rainbow of autumnal colours. Hearty enough as lunch on its own and perfect as an accompaniment to the Baked Chicken on page 116.

CRUNCHY BULGUR SALAD

250 g/1½ cups medium or coarse bulgur

200 g/7 oz. (about 1 small) fennel bulb, trimmed and finely diced

freshly squeezed juice and grated zest of ½ lemon

200 g/1½ cups (about 4 sticks) celery, thinly sliced on a diagonal

100 g/¾ cup dried pitted dates, roughly chopped

½ small radicchio, cored and leaves finely shredded

75 g/¾ cup walnuts, roughly chopped

20 g/scant ½ cup flat-leaf parsley, roughly chopped

20 g/scant ½ cup fresh mint, roughly chopped

sea salt and freshly ground black pepper, to season

DRESSING

1 garlic clove

2 teaspoons pomegranate molasses

50 ml/3 tablespoons olive oil

1 teaspoon sea salt

1 teaspoon ground cinnamon

SERVES 6

Begin by making the dressing. Crush the garlic to a paste with the salt in a pestle and mortar. Transfer to a small mixing bowl and whisk with the remaining ingredients. Cover and set aside.

Put the bulgur in a separate large mixing bowl. Add just enough boiling water to wet the grains but not go above the surface. Cover with clingfilm/plastic wrap and set aside for 15–20 minutes, until just tender but still with a bit of bite. Drain off any excess moisture using a fine mesh sieve/strainer, if necessary.

Place the diced fennel in another large mixing bowl and dress immediately with the lemon juice and zest to prevent any discolouration. Add the remaining ingredients and the soaked bulgur.

Pour over the prepared dressing and season with extra salt and pepper, to taste. Serve on a large plate with salad spoons.

A seriously addictive and healthy salad that makes a perfect dinner on a warm summer evening. If you don't have time to poach the chicken yourself, shred the meat from a store-bought barbecue chicken or a Peking duck from Chinatown.

ASIAN CHICKEN NOODLE SALAD

400 ml/1⅔ cups coconut milk

freshly squeezed juice and grated zest of 1 lime

700 g/1½ lbs. (about 5) chicken breasts

1 tablespoon palm sugar

500 g/18 oz. vermicelli glass noodles

100 g/1¾ cups beansprouts

30 g/generous ½ cup coriander/cilantro, chopped

30 g/generous ½ cup fresh mint, chopped

2 carrots, cut into matchsticks

1 cucumber, halved, deseeded and cut into matchsticks

4 spring onions/scallions, finely sliced

1 long red chilli/chile deseeded and cut into thin strips

50 g/½ cup peanuts, toasted (optional)

75 g/¾ cup fried crispy shallots (optional)

DRESSING

1 fresh red chilli/chile, deseeded and finely chopped

1 garlic clove, crushed

4 tablespoons fish sauce

2 tablespoons palm sugar

2 tablespoons freshly squeezed lime juice

2 teaspoons soy sauce

SERVES 6

Begin by poaching the chicken. Combine the coconut milk, lime juice and zest in a saucepan or pot big enough to hold the chicken breasts in one layer. Set over a medium heat, until bubbles start to appear on the surface. Add the chicken to the pan and bring to the boil. Immediately reduce the heat and gently simmer for about 10 minutes, until the chicken is just cooked.

Lift the chicken breasts out of the pan using a slotted spoon and place on a baking sheet to cool. Set the poaching liquid to one side.

To make the dressing, pound the chilli/chile and garlic to a paste in a pestle and mortar. Add the remaining ingredients, mix then set aside.

Place the noodles in a bowl and cover with boiling hot water. Set aside to soak for about 15 minutes.

When the chicken is cool, shred the meat finely and add 60 ml/¼ cup of the reserved poaching liquid to keep it moist.

Drain the noodles using a colander and place in a large serving bowl. Add the shredded chicken, beansprouts, coriander/cilantro, mint, carrot, cucumber, spring onions/scallions and chilli/chile. Pour over a little of the dressing and use your hands to mix everything together.

Top the salad with the toasted nuts and fried shallots, if desired, and serve with the remaining dressing on the side.

CAFÉ CULTURE

'Once you find a café you love you go again and again because it makes the city feel smaller; to feel the warmth of people who recognize you, know your name and know what coffee you drink.'

ALBERTO, LANTANA REGULAR

Not everyone is lucky enough to have a fantastic local café on their doorstep. Somewhere welcoming that smells of freshly ground coffee and delicious food being prepared, where the staff greet you by name, and the personality and passion of the owner is stamped on every lampshade, piece of crockery and each item on the menu.

When I first moved to London, I was struck by how few good independent cafés there were and instead, how corporate, homogenous chain cafés and coffee shops dominated the high street. Customers would bustle in and out, head down, absorbed in their own world, eager to get their coffee as quickly as possible and be on their way. This has changed dramatically in the last ten years, as more and more unique, quirky cafés have emerged – a testament to London's coffee house history.

In the 17th century after the Great Fire of London destroyed the Royal Exchange building, coffee houses became de facto trading houses and community hubs. People from all walks of life would sit at communal tables and talk, sharing ideas and engaging in political and intellectual debate. Coffee houses were an integral part of both working and social life.

I see this coffee house culture first hand at our cafés with our eclectic customer base. Whether it's friends catching up, local workers holding meetings, freelancers with laptops sharing a table with other freelancers using the café as a temporary office space, couples enjoying a leisurely brunch together, people reading the newspaper in the sunshine, or strangers chatting to each other as they wait for a coffee to take away. There's a relaxed but vibrant community atmosphere and a sense that people are coming here for something more than just the food and coffee.

When you find a good café it becomes an extension of your home and, in the words of one of our regulars, the city becomes a little smaller.

Two salads, perfect for any occasion: the ultimate potato salad with salty bacon and a creamy mayonnaise dressing; and mushrooms, greens and pesto – yum!

NEW POTATOES WITH BACON & MUSTARD MAYO

1 kg/2¼ lbs. new potatoes
200 g/1½ cups streaky bacon
20 g/scant ½ cup chives, finely chopped
20 g/scant ½ cup flat-leaf parsley, finely chopped

MUSTARD MAYO
1 egg
1 garlic clove, crushed
2 tablespoons white wine vinegar
½ teaspoon caster/granulated sugar
1 tablespoon grainy mustard
2 tablespoons hot English mustard
½ teaspoon sea salt
300 ml/1¼ cups olive or sunflower oil

a baking sheet lined with baking parchment

SERVES 6–8

Preheat the oven to 180°C (350°F) Gas 4.

Place the potatoes in a large saucepan or pot of salted water and bring to the boil over a medium–high heat. Cook for 20–25 minutes, until the potatoes are tender. Drain and set aside to cool. When cool enough to handle, cut in half.

Lay the bacon on the prepared baking sheet and cook in the preheated oven for 15–20 minutes, until really crisp. Remove from the oven and drain on paper towels. Chop into pieces, keeping the pieces quite large.

To make the Mustard Mayo, place all the ingredients except the oil in a food processor and blend. With the motor running, add the oil in a slow, steady drizzle until thick and pale in colour.

Mix the mustard mayo with the potatoes in a serving dish. Add the chopped herbs and bacon, and gently stir to combine.

MUSHROOM, PEAS, & SPINACH WITH HERB PESTO

3 tablespoons olive oil
1 garlic clove, sliced
8 portobello or large flat mushrooms
350 g/3 cups frozen peas, defrosted
80 g/1½ cups baby spinach
3 tablespoons pine nuts/kernels, toasted

HERB PESTO
20 g/scant ¼ cup pine nuts/kernels
10 g/scant ¼ cup fresh basil
20 g/1 cup fresh mint
½ garlic clove, grated
1 tablespoon freshly squeezed lemon juice
½ teaspoon grated lemon zest
25 g/⅓ cup grated Parmesan
3 tablespoons olive oil
½ teaspoon sea salt
freshly ground black pepper

SERVES 4–6

Preheat the oven to 180°C (350°F) Gas 4.

To prepare the mushrooms, heat the oil in a small saucepan or pot set over a medium heat. Add the sliced garlic and cook gently for 2 minutes. Arrange the whole mushrooms, stalk-side up, on a baking sheet. Spoon the oil and cooked garlic over the mushrooms, cover with foil and cook in the preheated oven for 10 minutes. Remove the foil and cook for another 15–20 minutes, or until the mushrooms are tender. Remove from the oven and set aside to cool.

To make the Herb Pesto, place all of the ingredients in a food processor and blend.

Slice the baked mushrooms into ½ cm/¼-inch pieces and put in a large mixing bowl with the defrosted peas and herb pesto. Add the baby spinach and toss everything together. Sprinkle the toasted pine nuts/kernels on top and serve.

If I had to choose a desert island luxury item it would be a mandolin as it is one of my most prized and well used tools in the kitchen. Using a mandolin to slice vegetables will transform your salads – courgettes/zucchini, beetroot/beets, fennel and carrots are all delicious raw when thinly sliced and dressed simply with lemon juice and olive oil.

SHAVED FENNEL SALAD WITH WALNUTS, PARMESAN & POMEGRANATE

4 tablespoons olive oil, plus extra to serve
3 tablespoons freshly squeezed lemon juice
grated zest of 1 lemon
15 g/¼ cup chopped chives
½ teaspoon sea salt
freshly ground black pepper, to season
600 g/1¼ lbs. (about 2 medium) fennel bulbs, trimmed and finely sliced

1 pear, cored, quartered and thinly sliced
seeds of 1 pomegranate
60 g/⅔ cup walnuts, toasted
60 g/1 cup Parmesan shavings
70 g/1¼ cup rocket/arugula

SERVES 6

Begin by whisking the oil together with the lemon juice and zest in a large mixing bowl. Add the chopped chives, salt and pepper to taste.

Add the sliced fennel and pear, and gently toss in the dressing to prevent any discolouration.

Add the remaining ingredients, one at a time, and gently mix together.

Serve with an extra drizzle of olive oil.

If the thought of pasta salad makes you recoil with images of cold pasta mixed with canned corn, drowned in mayo, fear not – this fresh, vibrant salad bears no resemblance.

ORZO WITH ROAST COURGETTES & SEMI-DRIED TOMATO DRESSING

250 g/4 cups orzo
   pasta
400 g/12 oz. (about 2)
   courgettes/
   zucchinis, cut in half
   lengthways
70 g/²/₃ cup feta
70 g/²/₃ cup black
   olives, pitted and
   halved
20 g/scant ½ cup flat-
   leaf parsley, chopped
sea salt and freshly
   ground black pepper,
   to season, plus extra
   for the dressing

DRESSING
1 bulb of garlic
125 ml/½ cup olive oil,
   plus 2 teaspoons
   to roast
80 g/¾ cup semi-dried
   tomatoes in oil,
   drained
¼ teaspoon caster/
   granulated sugar
1 tablespoon balsamic
   vinegar

SERVES 6

Preheat the oven to 200°C (400°F) Gas 6.

Begin by making the dressing. Cut the top part off the top of the garlic head to expose the individual garlic cloves. Place the garlic head, cut-side down, onto a square piece of foil and drizzle with 2 teaspoons of olive oil. Lift the foil up around the garlic and place on a baking sheet. Roast in the preheated oven for 45 minutes. Remove from the oven, open the foil wrap and set aside to cool. When the garlic is cool enough to handle, squeeze the cloves out of the skin, coarsely chop the garlic flesh and discard the skin.

Reduce the oven temperature to 180°C (350°F) Gas 4.

Place 50 g/½ cup of the semi-dried tomatoes in a food processor with the remaining olive oil, sugar, vinegar, salt and pepper. Blend and pour into a large mixing bowl.

Roughly chop the remaining semi-dried tomatoes and stir through the oil mixture with the roasted garlic.

To prepare the orzo pasta, place it in a saucepan or pot of salted boiling water set over a medium heat. Bring to the boil and cook for about 8 minutes until al dente.

Drain well before transferring to the bowl with the dressing while still warm. Toss to coat the orzo.

Preheat a grill-pan over a medium heat and, when hot, grill the courgettes/zucchinis, flesh-side down for 2 minutes until marked. Transfer the courgettes/zucchinis skin-side down to a baking sheet, season with salt and pepper and cook in the still-warm oven for 10 minutes. Remove from the oven and cut on the diagonal at 2-cm/¾-inch intervals.

Add the courgettes/ zucchinis, feta, olives and parsley and stir. Add a final drizzle of olive oil and serve.

Kohlrabi is a German word derived from 'Kohl', meaning cabbage and 'Rabi' meaning turnip and that is exactly what it tastes like, a cross between a turnip and a cabbage. This is a pretty little salad with the different shades of light green flecked with black poppy seeds.

KOHLRABI & SPROUT SLAW WITH HAZELNUTS

500 g/5 cups Brussels sprouts, finely sliced
500 g/18 oz. kohlrabi, peeled, quartered and thinly sliced
100 g/¾ cup (about 2 sticks) celery, thinly sliced on a diagonal
150 g/1½ cups (about 1 medium) green apples, peeled, cored and thinly sliced
20 g/scant ½ cup fresh mint, roughly chopped
20 g/scant ½ cup fresh chervil, roughly chopped
80 g/¾ cup roasted and peeled hazelnuts, chopped

DRESSING
1 teaspoon English mustard
60 ml/¼ cup apple cider vinegar
125 ml/½ cup extra virgin olive oil
2 tablespoon maple syrup
2 tablespoon crème fraîche
1 tablespoon poppy seeds
sea salt and freshly ground black pepper, to season

SERVES 2–4

This slaw is really easy to make. Place all the salad ingredients in a large mixing bowl and toss to combine.

To make the dressing, put all the ingredients into a bowl and whisk to combine. Adjust the seasoning to taste.

Add the dressing to the slaw and toss to coat all of the ingredients before serving.

GREEN BEAN & TOASTED CORN SALAD WITH SWEET MISO DRESSING

2 tablespoons vegetable oil, for frying
2 cobs of corn, peeled
300 g/2¼ green beans, ends trimmed
2 baby gem lettuce, washed and cut into 3-cm/1¼-inch rounds
25 g/½ cup coriander/ cilantro, roughly chopped
½ long red chilli/chile, deseeded and cut into fine rounds
1 tablespoon sesame seeds, toasted

DRESSING
1½ tablespoons white miso paste
3 tablespoons vegetable oil
2 teaspoons sesame oil
1 tablespoon rice wine vinegar
1½ tablespoons mirin or 1 tablespoon caster/granulated sugar
1 tablespoon freshly squeezed lemon juice
1 teaspoon grated lemon zest
1 garlic clove, crushed
¼ teaspoon sea salt

SERVES 2–4

Heat the oil in a frying pan/skillet set over a medium heat and add the corn. Cook for 8–10 minutes, turning occasionally until lightly charred in parts and tender. Remove from the pan and set aside to cool. When the corn is cool enough to handle, stand it on its end on a chopping board and run a sharp knife down the sides to remove the corn kernels from the cores. Transfer the corn to a large mixing bowl and discard the cores.

For the Sweet Miso Dressing, place all of the ingredients in a clean, screw top jar and shake well to combine.

Set a large saucepan or pot of salted water over a medium–high heat and bring to the boil. Blanch the beans in the water for 2–3 minutes, drain and set aside to cool.

Add the beans, lettuce, coriander/cilantro and chilli/chile to the corn and gently toss together. Add enough dressing to just coat the vegetables and toss together. Sprinkle with toasted sesame seeds and serve.

These three ingredients are made for each other. I love the comforting simplicity of this soup but if you wanted to spice it up a little you could add sliced red chilli/chile and some chopped fresh coriander/cilantro to serve.

SWEET POTATO,
COCONUT & GINGER SOUP

3 tablespoons olive oil

150 g/1 cup (about 1 medium) finely diced red onion

150 g/1 cup (about 3 sticks) chopped celery

1 leek, washed, trimmed and sliced

50 g/3½ tablespoons butter

5 garlic cloves, sliced

4 x 5-cm/2-in pieces of ginger, peeled and sliced

1 kg/2¼ lbs. (about 3 medium) sweet potatoes, peeled and thickly sliced

1¼ litres/5 cups vegetable stock

1 x 400-ml/14-oz. can coconut milk

sea salt and freshly ground black pepper, to season

seeded bread rolls, to serve

SERVES 6–8

Heat the oil in a heavy-bottomed saucepan or pot set over a medium heat. Add the onion, celery and leek, and cook for about 10 minutes.

Add the butter to the pan and allow it to melt before adding the garlic and ginger. Continue to sauté the mixture for another 5 minutes.

Add the sweet potato and pour in the stock.

Bring the mixture to the boil, cover and reduce the heat. Simmer for about 15 minutes or until the sweet potatoes are soft.

Remove the pan from the heat, add the coconut milk and purée with a handheld electric mixer or blend in a food processor.

Season to taste and serve with seeded bread rolls to dip in.

Tomato and basil are a classic summer flavour combination. The green basil oil provides a vibrant colour contrast to the orange-red of the soup base and elevates this humble tomato soup to something a little more refined.

TOMATO SOUP WITH FENNEL, GARLIC & BASIL DRIZZLE

1 bulb of garlic
olive oil, for roasting
350 g/10 oz. (about
    1 large) fennel bulb,
    trimmed and
    quartered
sea salt and freshly
    ground black pepper,
    to season
1 leek (white part only),
    roughly chopped
100 g/^{3}/$_4$ cup (about
    2 sticks) chopped
    celery
150 g/1^1/$_4$ cup (about
    1 medium) chopped
    carrot
500 g/2^1/$_2$ cups (about
    4 medium) roughly
    chopped tomatoes
1 x 400-g/14-oz. can
    plum tomatoes
500 ml/2 cups
    vegetable stock
15 g/^{1}/$_4$ cup fresh basil

BASIL OIL
150 ml/^{2}/$_3$ cup olive oil,
    plus extra if needed
60 g/1 cup fresh basil
sea salt, to taste

SERVES 4

Preheat the oven to 200°C (400°F) Gas 6.

To roast the garlic, cut the top part off the top of the garlic head to expose the individual garlic cloves. Place the garlic head, cut-side down, onto a square piece of foil and drizzle with 2 teaspoons of olive oil. Lift the foil up around the garlic and place on a baking sheet. Roast in the preheated oven for 45 minutes. Remove from the oven, open the foil wrap and set aside to cool. When the garlic is cool enough to handle, squeeze the cloves out of the skin, coarsely chop the garlic flesh and discard the skin.

Place the quartered fennel in a roasting pan, drizzle with 1 tablespoon of olive oil and season with the salt and freshly ground black pepper. Cook in the same oven as the garlic for 25 minutes, or until you can easily insert the tip of a sharp knife into the flesh. Remove from the oven, set aside to cool slightly then roughly chop.

To make the Basil Oil, whizz together a little of the olive oil with the fresh basil and salt in a food processor. With the motor running, slowly drizzle in more oil until you have a loose, flavoured oil. Set aside until ready to serve.

Heat 2 tablespoons of olive oil in a large saucepan or pot set over a medium heat. Add the chopped leek, celery and carrot and gently cook for 10–15 minutes, stirring from time to time, until the vegetables are soft.

Add the roast garlic and fennel, fresh and canned tomatoes and vegetable stock. Bring the mixture to the boil then reduce the heat and simmer for 45 minutes.

Remove the pan from the heat, stir in the basil leaves and purée with a handheld electric mixer or in a food processor.

Season to taste and serve with a good drizzle of basil oil, some freshly ground black pepper, and garnish with fresh basil leaves.

If you are one of those people who think that soup is not a proper meal, this is the soup that will change your mind. It's hearty and generous with meltingly tender lamb. I like the pearl barley with a bit of bite which is why I add it last.

LAMB SHANK BROTH WITH PEARL BARLEY

25 g/1¾ tablespoons butter

50 ml/3 tablespoons olive oil

150 g/1 cup (about 1 medium) finely diced red onion

200 g/1 cup (about 3 sticks) finely diced celery

1 leek, finely diced

380 g/2½ cups (about 2 medium) peeled and finely diced carrots

3 bay leaves

1½ teaspoons fennel seeds

1½ teaspoons dried oregano

4 garlic cloves, thinly sliced

1 teaspoon sea salt

175 g/1 cup pearl barley

50 g/1 cup flat-leaf parley, roughly chopped

25 g/½ cup fresh mint, roughly chopped

BRAISED LAMB

1½ kg/3¼ oz. (about 4) lamb shanks

150 g/1 cup (about 1 medium) finely diced red onion

150 g/1¼ cup (about 1 medium) chopped carrot

½ leek, trimmed and thickly sliced

100 g/¾ cup (about 2 sticks) chopped celery

1 teaspoon black peppercorns

3 bay leaves

3 sprigs thyme

2 sprigs rosemary

1 teaspoon dried oregano

SERVES 8

Begin by braising the lamb. Place the shanks in a heavy-bottomed saucepan or pot with the chopped vegetables, pepper and herbs. Cover with 2½ litres/10 cups of water, set the pan over a medium–high heat and bring to the boil. Reduce the heat and simmer for 2 hours, or until the lamb is tender and falling off the bone.

Lift the lamb from the pan using tongs or a slotted spoon and set on a plate to cool. When the lamb is cool enough to handle, shred the meat from the bones and cut any larger pieces into bite-sized pieces. Cover and set aside.

Strain the cooking liquor with a fine, mesh sieve or strainer set over a large mixing bowl. Discard the vegetables and reserve the liquid.

Melt the butter and oil together in a heavy-bottomed saucepan or pot set over a medium heat. Add the onion, celery, leek, carrots, bay leaves, fennel seeds and oregano. Toss the vegetables in the buttery oil.

Add the sliced garlic and gently sauté for 10–15 minutes, until the vegetables are soft.

Add the reserved cooking liquid from the lamb, salt and the pearl barley. Turn up the heat and bring the mixture to the boil. Add the shredded lamb, reduce the heat and simmer for about 15 minutes, until the pearl barley is cooked.

Add the chopped parsley and mint and serve in bowls.

A perfect soup for the spring and summer months when watercress is in season and you are craving lighter, fresher flavours. This soup is great cold too for when it gets really hot.

WATERCRESS, NEW POTATO & GARLIC SOUP

2 tablespoons olive oil
1 leek, roughly chopped
150 g/1 cup (about 3 sticks) chopped celery
3 sprigs thyme
1 sprig rosemary
1 bay leaf
5 garlic cloves, sliced
40 g/3 tablespoons butter
1¼ litres/5 cups vegetable stock
500 g/generous 1 cup new potatoes
350 g/7 cups fresh watercress, washed and trimmed
45 g/3 tablespoons crème fraîche, to serve

SERVES 4

Heat the oil in a heavy-bottomed saucepan or pot set over a medium heat. Add the leek and celery, and cook gently for about 5 minutes, until starting to soften.

Tie the thyme, rosemary and bay leaf together with some undyed kitchen twine to make a *bouquet garni*. Add the *bouquet garni* to the pan with the garlic and cook for 1 minute before adding the butter.

Continue to sauté the vegetables for 10 minutes, until well-cooked, completely soft, but not coloured.

Add the stock and new potatoes and bring the mixture to the boil. Reduce the heat, cover and simmer for 15–20 minutes, until the potatoes are soft and cooked through.

Add the watercress and stir through. Cover again, remove the pan from the heat and let the watercress wilt for 5 minutes.

Purée with a handheld electric mixer or blend in a food processor, until smooth.

Season to taste and serve in bowls with a dollop of crème fraîche stirred through each bowl.

The spicy Asian flavours and sweet fresh mango salsa set this succulent pork burger apart from a traditional beef burger, and makes a lighter alternative too.

SPICY PORK BURGER WITH MANGO SALSA

45 ml/3 tablespoons olive oil

115 g/¾ cup (about 1 small) finely diced onion

3 garlic cloves, crushed

a 4-cm/1½-in. piece of ginger, peeled and finely grated

900 g/2 lbs. minced/ground pork

2 long red chillies/chiles, deseeded and finely chopped

1 tablespoon fish sauce

2 tablespoons chopped coriander/cilantro

60 g/2 oz. bacon

2 eggs

sea salt and freshly ground black pepper, to season

MANGO SALSA

2 mangos, peeled, pitted and very finely diced

1 long fresh red chilli/chile, deseeded and finely diced

1 tablespoon chopped coriander/cilantro

1 tablespoon roughly chopped mint leaves

½ medium red onion, finely diced

freshly squeezed juice of 1 lime

2 teaspoons palm sugar

FENNEL & MINT SLAW

2 heaped tablespoons mayonnaise

freshly squeezed juice and grated zest of 1 lemon

200 g/7 oz. (about 1 small) fennel bulb, trimmed and sliced into rings

a bunch of fresh mint

40 g/scant 1 cup flat-leaf parsley

40 g/1½ oz. rocket/arugula

½ red onion, finely sliced

TO SERVE

6 burger buns

mayonnaise

SERVES 6

To make the Mango Salsa, mix all of the ingredients together in a bowl and set aside.

To make the slaw, mix the mayonnaise with the lemon juice and zest and then dress the fennel straight away to prevent the fennel discolouring. Gently mix through the herbs, rocket/arugula and the red onion.

For the burgers, heat 1 tablespoon of the oil in a frying pan/skillet and sauté the onion, garlic and ginger over a gentle heat until soft. Remove from the heat and allow to cool.

Place the remaining ingredients in a large bowl, add the onion mixture and combine. Season with salt and pepper.

Form into 6 burger patties (about 180 g/6½ oz. each). Refrigerate until ready to cook.

Preheat the oven to 170°C (325°F) Gas 3.

Heat the remaining 2 tablespoons of oil in a large frying pan/skillet and fry the burger patties for 4 minutes, turning once, until nice and brown on both sides. You may need to do this in batches, depending on the size of your pan/skillet.

Transfer the patties to a baking sheet and finish off in the oven for a further 10 minutes.

While the patties are cooking, lightly toast the burger buns. Spread some mayonnaise on the bottom bun and top with the pork pattie, mango salsa and the other half of the bun. Serve with the Fennel & Mint Slaw on the side.

We serve our brisket sandwich without a lid – it seems a shame to hide the glistening salt beef and beautiful pickles under a slice of bread. You can also serve it on a bagel.

BEEF BRISKET WITH HOMEMADE PICKLES

Place the rinsed raw brisket in a large pot with the onion, carrot, celery, garlic, rosemary, thyme, bay leaves and peppercorns. Cover with fresh, cold water and set over a high heat.

Bring the water to the boil then reduce the heat and gently simmer for 2–3 hours until the beef is cooked but still holding together. Remove the brisket from the stock and set aside to cool completely before slicing thinly, ensuring the cuts are made across the grain of the meat.

To make the Homemade Pickles, first prepare the Pickling Liquid. Place all the ingredients in a saucepan or pot with 125 ml/½ cup of water. Set over a medium–high heat and bring to the boil, stirring to ensure the sugar dissolves. Reduce the heat and simmer for 15 minutes, then remove from the heat, cover and set aside overnight to allow the flavours to infuse.

Toss the shredded cabbage in a good amount of salt and place in the fridge overnight.

The next day, reheat the Pickling Liquid and rinse the salted cabbage. Pat dry with a clean kitchen towel. Mix with the sliced carrot and chilli/chile and place in sterilized, glass jars. Pour over the hot pickling liquid so that the vegetables are completely submerged, then seal and store following the instructions on page 17.

To serve, toast the rye bread and spread each slice generously with mustard mayonnaise. Place some rocket/arugula on the bread and layer the salt beef over the bread. Take the pickled vegetables out of their pickling liquid, drain on paper towels and place in a bowl with the parsley and fennel flour. Toss to combine and place on top of each sandwich.

2½ kg/5½ lbs. raw salt beef brisket, rinsed
150 g/1 cup (about 1 medium) quartered red onion
200 g/1½ cups (about 1 large) chopped carrot
100 g/¾ cup (about 2 sticks) celery, halved
6 garlic cloves
25 g/scant ½ cup fresh rosemary needles
10 g/scant ¼ cup fresh thyme leaves
3 bay leaves
1 teaspoon black peppercorns

PICKLING LIQUID
250 g/1¼ cups caster/granulated sugar
500 ml/2 cups white wine vinegar
1 cinnamon stick
4 whole cloves
2 star anise
2 teaspoons coriander seeds
2 teaspoons fennel seeds
2 teaspoons black peppercorns

HOMEMADE PICKLES
450 g/4½ cups (about ½ small) finely shredded red cabbage
sea salt
300 g/2½ cups (about 2 medium) julienne-sliced carrot
1 long red chilli/chile, julienne-sliced

TO ASSEMBLE
12–16 slices light rye bread
mustard mayonnaise
50 g/1 cup rocket/arugula
30 g/½ cup flat-leaf parsley
1 teaspoon fennel flour/black onion seeds

sterilized, glass jars with airtight lids

SERVES 6–8

90 g/6 tablespoons cold unsalted butter, cut into small pieces
180 g/1½ cups plain/all-purpose flour
a pinch of sea salt
2–3 tablespoons ice-cold water

FILLING
20 g/4 teaspoons butter
2–3 leeks, trimmed and thinly sliced on a diagonal
7 eggs
250 ml/1 cup double/heavy cream
200 g/¾ cup crème fraîche
sea salt and freshly ground black pepper, to season
130 g/1⅔ cups grated Parmesan
80 g/1⅓ cup rocket/arugula

a 21-cm/8-in round, deep, fluted tart pan
baking beans
SERVES 8–10

Every day on the takeaway counter we have a selection of lusciously creamy, freshly baked tarts. The fillings vary but this one is a trusted favourite. The recipe requires a deep pan as there is nothing more disappointing than a thin, mean looking tart.

LEEK, ROCKET & PARMESAN TART

Preheat the oven to 190°C (375°F) Gas 5.

Place the butter, flour and salt in a food processor and pulse the mixture for 20–30 seconds, until it resembles coarse breadcrumbs. With the motor running, add the ice-cold water slowly and stop as soon as the dough comes together. It is important not to over mix the dough as it will become tough and if you add too much water it will shrink as it cooks. Wrap the dough in clingfilm/plastic wrap and chill in the fridge for at least 30 minutes before using.

Roll the dough out as thinly as possible on a lightly floured surface. Line the tart pan with the pastry and prick the base all over with a fork. Place the pan on a baking sheet, line with a piece of greased baking parchment slightly larger than the pan and fill the case with baking beans.

Bake in the preheated oven for 15–20 minutes. Remove the baking beans and parchment and return the pastry case to the oven to cook for a further 5–10 minutes, or until it is pale golden and cooked through. Remove from the oven and set aside to cool.

Reduce the heat to 160°C (325°F) Gas 3.

Melt the butter in a large saucepan or pot set over a medium heat. Add the leeks and sweat until soft but avoid browning.

In a large mixing bowl, whisk together the eggs, cream and crème fraîche. Season with salt and pepper, then gently stir in the Parmesan, cooked leeks and rocket/arugula.

Pour the mixture into the cooled tart case, making sure the leeks and rocket/arugula are evenly distributed.

Cook for about 1 hour in the still-warm oven, until golden and just set. Serve hot or cold.

The relish for this dish was inspired by a meal I had at one of my favourite restaurants in London. They served their relish with barbecued quail but because cheese and fruit is such a classic pairing, I think it works really well with the Baked Ricotta.

BAKED RICOTTA WITH AUBERGINE, CURRANT & PINE NUT RELISH

1 kg/5 cups ricotta
1 garlic clove
½ teaspoon sea salt
2 eggs, separated
1 teaspoon grated
   lemon zest
1 tablespoon thyme
   leaves
60 g/1 cup grated
   Parmesan

RELISH
800 g/6 cups (about
   2 large) diced
   aubergine/eggplant
125 ml/½ cup red wine
250 ml/1 cup balsamic
   vinegar
½ star anise
1 tablespoon caster/
   granulated sugar
125 ml/½ cup
   sunflower oil
1 tablespoon currants
3 tablespoons pine
   nuts/kernels,
   toasted
2 tablespoons chopped
   flat-leaf parsley

6 x 250-ml/1-cup
   capacity ramekins,
   greased

SERVES 6

Preheat the oven to 200°C (400°F) Gas 6.

Drain the ricotta in a fine mesh sieve/strainer and put in a large mixing bowl. Pound the garlic with the salt in a pestle and mortar. Stir the garlic paste through the ricotta together with the egg yolks, lemon zest, thyme and grated Parmesan.

In a separate large mixing bowl, whisk the egg whites to soft peaks.

Add a large spoonful of the egg whites to the ricotta mixture and stir to loosen it. Gently fold in the remaining egg whites until just incorporated, then pour the mixture into the prepared ramekins.

Bake in the preheated oven for 20 minutes, until slightly golden on top and the cheese is just set. It will puff up slightly during cooking and deflate while cooling, so don't be alarmed. Allow the ricotta to cool completely before turning out onto serving plates.

Next, make the relish. Put the aubergine/eggplant in a large sieve/strainer set over a mixing bowl, sprinkle with salt and set aside for 20 minutes. Rinse, pat dry and set aside. Place the red wine, balsamic vinegar, star anise and sugar in a medium saucepan or pot set over a medium heat. Bring to the boil, then reduce the heat and simmer for about 15 minutes, until the liquid has reduced by two-thirds and become syrupy.

Meanwhile, heat the oil in a large frying pan/skillet over a medium heat. Shallow fry the aubergine/eggplant in batches until golden brown. Add extra oil as required. Drain the aubergine/eggplant on paper towels and set aside.

Remove the star anise from the red wine reduction. Add the currants and fried aubergine/eggplant, and simmer gently over a low heat with a lid on for 30 minutes – most of the liquid should be soaked up. Remove from the heat and stir in the pine nuts/kernels and parsley.

Season to taste and serve with the baked ricotta.

This is such a pretty salad with the different layers yielding many different flavours, colours and textures. It is also delicious with prawns/shrimp. Use peeled green ones with the tail on and grill them the same way as the squid.

GRILLED SQUID SALAD WITH HERB LIME DRESSING

2 red (bell) peppers
800 g/1¾ lbs. cleaned squid
2 heads of chicory, leaves removed and cut in half lengthways
30 g/½ cup baby spinach leaves
40 g/¼ cup edamame or broad beans (fresh or frozen), blanched
10 g/scant ¼ cup coriander/cilantro

DRESSING
freshly squeezed juice of 2 limes
30 ml/2 tablespoons olive oil
20 g/2 tablespoons palm sugar
1 garlic clove, grated
30 g/½ cup finely chopped coriander/cilantro
15 g/¼ cup finely chopped basil
30 ml/2 tablespoons fish sauce
1 long fresh red chilli/chile, deseeded and finely chopped
freshly ground black pepper, to season

a baking sheet, lined with foil

SERVES 4

Preheat the oven to 200°C (400°F) Gas 6.

Begin by roasting the red peppers. Place on the prepared baking sheet and roast in the preheated oven for 20 minutes. Turn and roast for a further 20 minutes until the peppers collapse and the skin is charred and soft. Transfer to a small mixing bowl, cover with clingfilm/plastic wrap and set aside. When the peppers are cool enough to handle, remove and discard the skin and seeds, and slice.

To make the herb lime dressing, combine all the ingredients in a small mixing bowl using a whisk. It is important to make the dressing by hand rather than using a blender as you want the dressing to have texture.

To prepare the squid, cut off but reserve the tentacles and cut down the 'seam' of the squid so it opens out flat. Score the inside with a cross-hatch pattern, then slice lengthways into 2-cm/¾-inch wide strips. Cut the tentacles in half and add to the squid strips.

Preheat a grill pan/skillet over a medium–high heat. Sear the squid and the tentacles for 1–2 minutes until curled up and slightly charred. Remove the pan from the heat and dress with 2 tablespoons of the herb lime dressing.

Layer the chicory, spinach, sliced roast peppers and edamame on a platter. Drizzle with the remaining dressing, and gently mix through. Place the grilled squid on top and garnish with the coriander/cilantro. Serve immediately.

I always like to be able to tell what flavour a tart is by looking at it. Here, with the asparagus floating on the surface like synchronised swimmers, there's no mistaking who's the star of the show.

ASPARAGUS, GOAT'S CHEESE
& SPINACH TART

90 g/6 tablespoons cold unsalted butter, cut into small pieces
180 g/1½ cups plain/all-purpose flour
a pinch of sea salt
2–3 tablespoons ice-cold water

FILLING
7 eggs
250 ml/1 cup double/heavy cream
200 g/¾ cup crème fraîche
12 asparagus spears, ends removed
150 g/1½ cups goat's cheese
80 g/1⅓ cup baby spinach leaves

a 21-cm/8-in round, deep, fluted tart pan
baking beans

SERVES 8–10

Preheat the oven to 190°C (375°F) Gas 5.

Place the butter, flour and salt in a food processor and pulse the mixture for 20–30 seconds, until it resembles coarse breadcrumbs. With the motor running, add the ice-cold water slowly and stop as soon as the dough comes together. It is important not to over mix the dough as it will become tough and if you add too much water it will shrink as it cooks. Wrap the dough in clingfilm/plastic wrap and chill in the fridge for at least 30 minutes before using.

Roll the dough out as thinly as possible on a lightly floured surface. Line the tart pan with the pastry and prick the base all over with a fork. Place on a baking sheet, line with a piece of greased baking parchment slightly larger than the pan and fill with baking beans.

Bake in the preheated oven for 15–20 minutes. Remove the baking beans and parchment and return the pastry case to the oven to cook for a further 5–10 minutes, or until it is pale golden and cooked through. Remove from the oven and set aside to cool. Reduce the heat to 160°C (325°F) Gas 3.

In a large mixing bowl, whisk together the eggs, cream and crème fraîche. Season with salt and pepper, then gently stir in the goat's cheese and spinach.

Pour the mixture into the cooled tart case, making sure the cheese and spinach are evenly distributed.

Lay the asparagus spears in a single layer on top of the egg mixture, alternating head and tail, and gently push them into the tart.

Cook for about 1 hour in the still-warm oven, until golden and just set. Serve hot or cold.

PRODUCE & INGREDIENTS

It staggers me when I hear statistics on the amount of food the average household throws out. My parents instilled in me an aversion to food wastage. When I was growing up, Sunday night presented a prime opportunity to transform the week's leftovers into dinner. As you can imagine this 'clearing out the fridge' approach to cooking had mixed results, but on the whole, they were tasty and satisfying dishes. Leftover meat became a curry, any combination of cooked vegetables were smothered in white sauce or breadcrumbs and baked, and there were endless risottos and pasta sauces.

While I don't think it was intentional, my parents' approach to cooking shaped the way I think about ingredients and recipes. It is all well and good to encourage people to eat seasonally and to buy local and organic ingredients. Equally as important is how resourceful we can be with the ingredients we have, to avoid wasting food or throwing food away because it has been forgotten about and left in the fridge to spoil.

It requires a spirit of adventure but I'd encourage you to treat recipes as a guide rather than a rigid set of instructions. Substitute ingredients with what you already have or what you can see is in season when you go shopping. Not only will you create new dishes and discover new flavour combinations, you will save money by not throwing food out and get better flavour (and value) from seasonal ingredients grown locally.

I always try to build a meal from something left over from the previous night. Over the course of a week, elements of meals become intertwined and leftovers provide inspiration for the next night's dinner. Leftover roast vegetables become bubble and squeak, leftover caponata becomes a pasta sauce, leftover baked chicken is shredded for a chicken noodle salad or leftover wild mushroom stew, topped with puff pastry is transformed into a pot pie.

This approach to using leftovers extends to the café as well. One of our most popular dishes was a 'rib-wich', created one day when we had an abundance of sticky Asian pork ribs from the dinner menu. The chef shredded the meat, crisped it on the grill and served it in a toasted ciabatta with hot sauce and aioli for lunch.

Our motto: resourcefulness is the mother of deliciousness.

LANTANA LUNCH

SOUP – WATERCRESS, NEW POTATO & GARLIC

HOT DISH – MAC N' CHEESE W/ HAM & SPINACH

CHICKEN – HONEY MUSTARD

SALMON – LEMON & THY...

TART – COURGETTE, SPINACH & ...
– HAM, CHEDDAR, WATERCRESS ... MUSTARD

SALADS – BEETROOT, ROAST CARROT, PEAS & ...
– BULGAR, CELERY, CHICORY & DA...
– FRISÉE, RED ONION, FETA & PARSLEY

It's always good to have an easy, one-pot stew in your repertoire and this is a delicious and rustic dish. The parsley and lemon zest added at the end gives it an extra flourish of flavour.

BRAISED CHICKEN WITH BACON, SAFFRON, TOMATO & POTATO

8–12 chicken thigh fillets, skin on
4 tablespoons olive oil
600 g/1 lb 5 oz. bacon lardons or thick-cut streaky bacon
700 g/6 cups (about 2) chopped onions
775 g/6 cups (about 4) peeled and diced carrots
300 g/1½ cups (about 2 sticks/ribs) diced celery
4 garlic cloves, crushed
1 teaspoon smoked paprika
1 fresh red chilli/chile, deseeded and finely chopped
200 ml/¾ cup red wine
2 x 400-g/14-oz. cans chopped tomatoes
400 ml/1½ cups chicken stock
a good pinch of saffron threads
1 kg/2 lb 4 oz. potatoes, peeled and cut into chunks
grated zest of 2 lemons
leaves from a small bunch of flat-leaf parsley, roughly chopped
sea salt and freshly ground black pepper, to season

SERVES 8–12

Season the chicken fillets with sea salt. Heat the olive oil in a large, deep frying pan/skillet set over a high heat. Add the chicken and fry until golden brown. Remove the chicken from the pan and set aside.

Add the bacon to the pan and fry over high heat for 2 minutes. Add the onions, carrots, celery, garlic, paprika and chilli/chile and stir well. Cover with a lid, reduce the heat slightly and cook for 5–10 minutes, until the vegetables have started to soften.

Stir in the wine and let it bubble for 2–3 minutes. Add the chopped tomatoes, stock and saffron and bring to a simmer. Allow the sauce to simmer and reduce for about 20 minutes.

Return the browned chicken fillets to the pan. Add the potatoes and the zest of 1 of the lemons, and simmer for a further 20 minutes, until the potato is cooked and the sauce has thickened.

Remove from the heat and stir through the chopped parsley and zest of the remaining lemon. Check the seasoning and adjust as required.

150 g/5 cups dried porcini mushrooms
5 fresh tomatoes
2 tablespoons olive oil, plus extra for frying
1 large onion, diced
1 tablespoon plain/all-purpose flour
150 ml/⅔ cup white wine
700 g/1 lb 9 oz. (about 6 caps) Portobello mushrooms, thickly sliced
350 g/5 cups button mushrooms, whole if very small or halved
200 g/3 cups oyster mushrooms, cut in half lengthways
2 teaspoons fresh thyme leaves
1 teaspoon dried chilli flakes/hot red pepper flakes
1 tablespoon tomato purée/paste
sea salt and freshly ground black pepper, to season

WALNUT GREMOLATA
50 g/½ cup walnuts
25 g/½ cup chopped flat-leaf parsley
1 garlic clove, crushed
grated zest of 1 lemon

SOFT POLENTA
200 g/1⅓ cups quick-cook polenta/cornmeal
80 g/5 tablespoons butter
100 g/½ cup finely grated Parmesan
1 teaspoon sea salt

SERVES 6

Osso buco, a classic Italian meat dish, is the unlikely inspiration for this rich vegetarian stew. It's so packed full of flavour you won't notice there isn't any meat involved.

MUSHROOM STEW WITH WALNUT GREMOLATA ON SOFT POLENTA

First make the gremolata. Put the walnuts on a baking sheet and roast in the oven at 170°C (325°F) Gas 3 for 5 minutes. When cool, chop finely, put in a small bowl and combine with the remaining ingredients. Season to taste and set aside until needed.

Put the porcini in a heatproof bowl and add 500 ml/2 cups boiling water. Set aside to soak.

Score the base of the tomatoes, put them in a heatproof bowl and add enough boiling water to cover. After 10 minutes remove them from the water, let cool then peel, deseed and chop the flesh. Set aside.

Heat 2 tablespoons of oil in a frying pan/skillet set over a medium heat. Add the onion and cook, stirring, for about 10 minutes, until the onion has softened but not coloured. Increase the heat and add the flour. Stir to incorporate and cook for 1 minute. Add the wine and let it bubble for 1 minute, deglazing the pan with a wooden spoon. Remove from the heat and set aside.

Heat 1 tablespoon of oil in a large frying pan/skillet set over a medium–high heat. Add the Portobello and button mushrooms in batches and fry until lightly brown, adding more oil between batches as necessary. Remove the pan from the heat while you drain the porcini and squeeze out excess liquid (reserving the soaking water for later).

Chop the porcini and add them to the other mushrooms in the pan, along with the oyster mushrooms. Add the reserved onion mixture, thyme, chilli/hot pepper flakes, tomato purée/paste, chopped fresh tomatoes and 375 ml/1½ cups of the reserved porcini soaking liquid. Return the pan to the heat and simmer gently for 20 minutes, until the sauce has thickened. Season to taste with salt and pepper.

To make the polenta, bring 1 litre/4 cups water to the boil in a medium saucepan and add the salt.

Pour in the polenta and stir constantly over a very gentle heat for about 10 minutes, until the polenta is coming away from the sides and is smooth in texture – watch out as it will splatter.

Add the butter and Parmesan, beat well to combine, taste and adjust the seasoning as required.

Pour the polenta into a serving dish, ladle on the mushroom stew and sprinkle with the Walnut Gremolata. Serve immediately.

Baked chicken is an ideal meal to prepare for a crowd. The legs can be eaten with your hands – perfect picnic fare.

BAKED CHICKEN THREE WAYS

6 chicken legs (cut in half into thigh and drumstick portions)
1 lemon or lime, cut into 8 wedges

CRACKED BLACK PEPPER & MAPLE
1 tablespoon black peppercorns
1 teaspoon sea salt
150 ml/^{2}/$_3$ cup pure maple syrup
35 ml/2 generous tablespoons olive oil

HONEY & MUSTARD
3^1/$_2$ tablespoons hot English mustard
2^1/$_2$ tablespoons wholegrain mustard
50 ml/scant ^{1}/$_4$ cup olive oil
100 g/^{1}/$_3$ cup clear honey

LEMONGRASS & GINGER
40 g/^{1}/$_2$ oz. garlic (about 10 cloves) peeled and roughly chopped
a 5-cm/2-inch piece of ginger, peeled and roughly chopped
2 stalks of lemongrass, white part only, roughly chopped
25 g/^{1}/$_2$ cup chopped coriander/cilantro (including stems)
25 ml/5 teaspoons soy sauce
50 ml/scant ^{1}/$_4$ cup sweet chilli sauce
45 ml/3 tablespoons vegetable oil

SERVES 6

Begin by preparing your desired marinade.

For the Cracked Black Pepper & Maple marinade, put the peppercorns into a mortar, and pound to a coarse consistency with a pestle. Transfer the pepper to a large mixing bowl and stir in the salt, syrup and oil. Set aside until you are ready to cook the chicken.

For the Honey & Mustard marinade, stir the mustards, oil and honey together in a large bowl.

For the Lemongrass & Ginger marinade, place all of the ingredients in a food processor and blitz for 2 minutes.

Put the chicken pieces into a large mixing bowl and coat well with your choice of marinade using your hands. Cover and set in the fridge to marinade for 2 hours, or overnight.

When ready to cook, preheat the oven to 160°C (325°F) Gas 3.

Put the chicken and lemon or lime wedges into a roasting pan big enough to accommodate the chicken in a single layer. Cover with foil and roast in the preheated oven for 1^1/$_2$ hours.

Remove the foil and increase the heat to 200°C (400°F) Gas 6. Cook for a further 20–30 minutes to get a good colour on the legs, taking care not to let them burn.

Remove from the oven and, using a pair of tongs, immediately turn the pieces of chicken over in the pan to allow the cooking juices to run through. Let cool slightly, then serve hot or cold.

Duck is an impressive meat to cook for friends as it's not a bird that people often cook for themselves. The sweet and sour dressing for the slaw balances the richness of the duck.

WARM DUCK BREAST WITH ROAST RED PEPPER, CABBAGE & KOHLRABI SLAW

6 duck breasts
1 tablespoon fennel
    seeds
1 tablespoon coriander
    seeds
2 teaspoons sea salt
450 g/6 cups (about
    ½ small) shredded
    red cabbage
250 g/3 cups (about ½)
    peeled and thinly
    sliced kohlrabi
150 g/1 heaped cup
    mange tout/snow
    peas, thinly sliced
    lengthways
30 g/⅔ cup roughly
    chopped coriander/
    cilantro
1 pomegranate

DRESSING
2 red (bell) peppers,
    deseeded and cut
    into quarters
olive oil, for roasting
1 shallot or ½ red
    onion, finely chopped
1 long fresh red
    chilli/chile, deseeded
    and finely chopped
1 garlic clove, crushed
2 tablespoons balsamic
    vinegar
1½ teaspoons sea salt
60 ml/¼ cup vegetable
    oil
sea salt and freshly
    ground black pepper,
    to season

SERVES 6

Begin by dry roasting the fennel and coriander seeds in a frying pan/skillet set over a medium heat for 1–2 minutes, until fragrant. Put in a mortar and use the pestle to crush them to a powder. Mix in the salt.

Pat the duck breasts dry with paper towels. Using a sharp knife, score the duck skin in a cross hatch pattern, taking care not to cut into the meat. Rub the spice mix all over the duck breasts using your hands. Cover with clingfilm/plastic wrap and put in the fridge for a couple of hours (overnight is ideal).

To make the roast red pepper dressing, preheat the oven to 180°C (350°F) Gas 4.

Toss the peppers in a little olive oil and season with salt and pepper. Put them on a baking sheet and roast in the preheated oven for around 35–40 minutes, until soft and the skins are blackening.

Remove from the oven and put in a bowl. Cover with clingfilm/plastic wrap and leave for 15 minutes. When cool enough to handle, peel off the skins and roughly chop the flesh. Put the roast peppers, shallot, garlic, chilli/chile, vinegar and salt in a blender with the vegetable oil. Blitz for 1–2 minutes until smooth. Set aside until ready to serve.

For the salad, remove the seeds of the pomegranate by cutting it in half and holding one half in your hand with the seeds facing your palm. Place your hand over a bowl and hit the back of the fruit with a wooden spoon. Remove any white membrane that falls into the bowl with the seeds. Repeat with the other half.

Put the red cabbage, kohlrabi, mange tout/snow peas, coriander/cilantro and pomegranate seeds together in a large bowl and toss. Add sufficient red pepper dressing to lightly coat the slaw.

Next preheat the oven to 190°C (375°F) Gas 5.

Sear the duck breasts skin-side down in a hot, heavy-based dry frying pan/skillet for about 3–5 minutes until the skin is golden brown on one side. (Do this in batches so as not to overcrowd your pan and pour off any fat in between batches). Turn the breasts over and sear on the other side for about 30 seconds. Transfer to a baking sheet and finish cooking in the preheated oven for about 10 minutes, until just pink. Remove from the oven, cover with kitchen foil and allow to rest for 5 minutes.

Serve the duck breasts whole or sliced on the diagonal with the slaw.

I love the versatility of traditionally cheaper cuts of meat that benefit from slow cooking – it's a great way to accommodate many flavours and styles. This is just one.

SLOW ROAST LAMB SHOULDER WITH KISIR, CHICKPEAS & CUMIN YOGURT DRESSING

1½ tablespoons ground cumin

1 tablespoon ground coriander

2½ kg/5 lb 8 oz. lamb shoulder on the bone

1 bulb of garlic, peeled and separated into cloves

2 carrots, diced

1 leek, diced

3 stalks celery, diced

1 tablespoon olive oil

2 x 400-g/14-oz. cans chopped tomatoes

375 ml/1½ cups white wine

2 bay leaves

1 cinnamon stick

2 x 400-g/14-oz. cans chickpeas, drained

2 tablespoons finely chopped preserved lemon skin

leaves from a small bunch of mint, finely chopped

sea salt and freshly ground black pepper, to season

KISIR

300 g/2 cups bulgur

1 tablespoon olive oil

1 teaspoon sea salt

400 g/14 oz. (about 1 head) cauliflower, broken into thumb-sized florets

20 g/scant ½ cup finely chopped coriander/cilantro

20 g/scant ½ cup finely chopped mint

40 g/scant 1 cup finely chopped flat-leaf parsley

4 spring onions/scallions, finely diced

60 g/½ cup shelled pistachio nuts

½ cucumber, deseeded and finely diced

4 fresh green chillies/chiles, finely diced

seeds of ½ a pomegranate

freshly squeezed juice and grated zest of 2 lemons

CUMIN YOGURT DRESSING

300 ml/1¼ cups Greek yogurt

1 teaspoon ground cumin

½ garlic clove, grated

1 tablespoon freshly squeezed lemon juice

SERVES 6–8

Rub the ground spices over the lamb. Using a small sharp knife, cut 2-cm/1-inch incisions in the lamb and push the garlic cloves deep into the holes so that they are encased. Let marinate for at least 30 minutes while you preheat the oven to 200°C (400°F) Gas 6.

Sauté the carrots, leek and celery in olive oil in a frying pan/skillet for 10 minutes. Transfer to a roasting pan. Add the lamb to the frying pan/skillet, increase the heat and brown the meat all over. Put the lamb on top of the vegetables in the roasting pan. Pour the tomatoes, wine and 250 ml/1 cup water over the lamb and tuck the bay leaves and cinnamon stick underneath. Season well and cover with kitchen foil.

Reduce the oven temperature to 160°C (325°F) Gas 3. Cook the lamb for 4–4½ hours, until it pulls away easily from the bone. Remove the pan from the oven, lift out the lamb and cover with kitchen foil. You may have oil on the surface of the vegetables. Use a large metal spoon to skim this off and discard. Remove the bay leaves and cinnamon stick. Transfer the vegetables to a blender and blitz until smooth. Check the seasoning and adjust if necessary. Put half the purée in a saucepan and add the chickpeas. Simmer for 20 minutes, until you have a thick gravy. Stir in the lemon and mint.

For the Kisir, put the bulgur in a large bowl with the olive oil and salt. Add 250 ml/1 cup boiling water, cover and set aside. Heat a heavy-based frying pan/skillet and dry fry the cauliflower in batches, until lightly charred. Add the cooled cauliflower and all the remaining ingredients to the bulgur and season to taste.

For the Cumin Yogurt Dressing, simply mix the ingredients together and season to taste.

Vincotto is a naturally sweet, 'cooked wine' syrup that can be used in both sweet and savoury dishes. It pairs beautifully with the salty halloumi cheese and earthy beetroot/beet in this salad. If you can't find vincotto you can substitute balsamic vinegar with a little honey. Like wine, vincottos vary a lot in quality so buy the best that you can find.

50 g/½ cup pecans, toasted
25 g/½ cup flat-leaf parsley
2 tablespoons olive oil
250 g/9 oz. halloumi, cut into 1-cm/⅜-in slices
freshly squeezed juice of ½ a lemon
sea salt and freshly ground black pepper, to season

ROAST BEETROOT
750 g/1 lb 9 oz. (about 4 medium) beetroots/beets
2 tablespoons olive oil
1 tablespoon vincotto (or 1 tablespoon each of balsamic vinegar and clear honey)
1 teaspoon fennel seeds

ROAST SHALLOTS
300 g/2 cups peeled and quartered shallots
1 tablespoon olive oil
½ tablespoon vincotto

DRESSING
2 teaspoons vincotto
2 tablespoons olive oil
1 teaspoon clear honey
1 garlic clove, crushed

SERVES 2

GRILLED HALLOUMI WITH ROAST SHALLOTS, BEETROOT & VINCOTTO

Begin by preparing the beetroots/beets. Put them in a saucepan or pot of boiling water and cook for about 40 minutes, until just tender. Drain and set aside to cool.

Once cold enough to handle, peel and cut into wedges.

Preheat the oven to 180°C (350°F) Gas 4.

Place the beetroot/beet wedges in a large mixing bowl with the oil, vincotto (or substitute) and fennel seeds. Toss to ensure everything is well-coated, then spread out on a baking sheet. Season with salt and pepper and roast in the preheated oven for 30 minutes.

Meanwhile, prepare the shallots. Place them in a large mixing bowl with the oil and vincotto (or substitute). Toss together and spread out on a baking sheet.

Season with salt and pepper and roast in the same oven for about 15 minutes, until soft.

To make the vincotto dressing, place the vincotto, oil, honey and crushed garlic in a clean screw-top jar. Close the jar and shake. Season with salt and pepper.

Place the roast beetroot/beets, roast shallots, pecans and parsley in a large mixing bowl and gently toss together with the dressing and set aside until ready to serve.

Heat the oil in a large frying pan/skillet and fry the halloumi slices for 2 minutes on each side, until golden brown. Remove from the pan and drain on paper towels.

Serve the roast vegetable salad in bowls with the halloumi arranged on top. Squeeze the lemon juice over the cheese and enjoy.

Low, slow cooking with Asian ingredients produces incredible flavours and this dish is one of my all-time favourites. The caramel is not too sweet and the pork literally melts in your mouth.

VIETNAMESE CARAMELISED PORK SHOULDER

4 aubergines/eggplant
olive oil, for roasting
sea salt and freshly
    ground black pepper,
    to season
90 g/scant $\frac{1}{2}$ cup
    caster/granulated
    sugar
500 g/3$\frac{1}{2}$ cups diced
    banana shallots
3 long fresh red
    chillies/chiles, cut
    into rings
4 garlic cloves, finely
    chopped
2 x 5-cm/2-inch pieces
    of ginger, peeled and
    finely grated
40 ml/3 tablespoons
    fish sauce
675 ml/2$\frac{2}{3}$ cups
    vegetable stock
2 star anise
1$\frac{1}{2}$ teaspoons coarse
    black pepper
1$\frac{1}{2}$ kg/3$\frac{1}{4}$ lbs. pork
    shoulder, cut into
    large chunks
6 spring onions/
    scallions, cut into
    2$\frac{1}{2}$-cm/1-in lengths
50 g/1 cup coriander/
    cilantro, roughly
    chopped
100 g/1$\frac{3}{4}$ cups
    beansprouts
steamed rice, to serve

SERVES 6

Preheat the oven to 180°C (350°F) Gas 4.

Cut the aubergines/eggplant in half lengthways and then in half again to create 4 long wedges. Cut each wedge into thirds across. Place on a baking sheet, drizzle generously with olive oil and season with salt and pepper. Roast in the preheated oven for about 15 minutes, until golden. Remove from the oven and set aside.

To make the caramel, put 60 g/$\frac{1}{3}$ cup of the sugar in a saucepan or pot set over a medium heat. Let the sugar melt, without stirring. Shake the pan every 5 minutes or so, until all the sugar has melted and it is the colour of dark, runny honey. It may take a while so be patient.

Remove the pan from the heat and add 100 ml/$\frac{1}{3}$ cup of warm water. (Watch out, it will splatter as it bubbles.) Stir with a wooden spoon, then set aside.

In a large, heavy-bottomed saucepan or pot big enough to hold the pork, fry the shallots, chillies/chiles, garlic and ginger until soft. Add the fish sauce and stir for 2–3 minutes.

Add the vegetable stock, roast aubergines/eggplant, caramel, star anise, black pepper, remaining sugar and the pork. Bring to the boil, then reduce the heat, cover with a lid and gently simmer for 2 hours. Remove the lid and continue to simmer for 45 minutes. Skim off and discard any fat on the surface with a large metal spoon.

Just before serving, stir though the spring onions/scallions. Garnish with the coriander/cilantro and beansprouts.

Serve in bowls with plenty of the cooking liquid and steamed rice on the side.

Beetroot/beet and blue cheese is a classic combination, one that works really well with beef which is strong enough to hold its own with these gutsy flavours. You could easily substitute burgers for the steak and serve them in a bun.

STEAK SANDWICH WITH BEETROOT JAM & BLUE CHEESE DRESSING

4 x 150-g/6-oz. rump
    steaks
olive oil
8 slices of sourdough
    bread
80 g/1⅔ cups
    watercress
2 large tomatoes,
    sliced

JAM/JELLY
500 g/3¼ cups
    roughly chopped
    beetroots/beets
50 g/4 tablespoons
    finely grated
    horseradish
100 ml/⅓ cup balsamic
    vinegar
50 g/¼ cup light brown
    sugar
1 teaspoon sea salt

DRESSING
60 g/¼ cup sour/
    soured cream
60 ml/¼ cup
    buttermilk
1 tablespoon freshly
    squeezed lemon juice
1 tablespoon chopped
    dill
½ teaspoon sea salt
freshly ground black
    pepper
100 g/¾ cup crumbled
    Stilton or other blue
    cheese

SERVES 4

Begin by preparing the jam/jelly. Put the beetroots/beets in a saucepan or pot of boiling water and cook for about 40 minutes, until just tender. Drain and set aside to cool.

Once cold enough to handle, peel and grate into a clean, large saucepan or pot.

Add the other ingredients, set the pan over a gentle heat and simmer for 30–40 minutes until there is no liquid and the beetroot/beets are of a jammy consistency. Remove from the heat and set aside or seal and store following the instructions on page 17.

To make the blue cheese dressing, put the sour/soured cream, buttermilk, lemon juice, dill, salt and pepper in a mixing bowl and mix well. Add the crumbled Stilton, stir through and set aside.

Rub the steaks with olive oil and season with salt and pepper.

Place a ridged grill pan/skillet over a high heat and get it really hot before placing the steaks on top. Cook for about 3 minutes on each side, then place on a plate and cover with foil to allow the meat to rest.

Lightly toast the sourdough bread and put a generous layer of jam/jelly on the bottom of 4 of the slices. Put the watercress over the jam/jelly, and top with some sliced tomato.

Slice the rested steaks on the diagonal into 1-cm/⅜-inch slices and arrange over the tomato.

Spoon some blue cheese dressing on top of the warm steak so that the cheese starts to melt and place the other slice of toasted bread on top.

700 g/7 cups (about 2) diced aubergine/eggplant

125 ml/½ cup olive oil

1 large onion, diced

1 garlic clove, crushed

1 red plus 1 orange or yellow (bell) pepper, deseeded and diced

2 celery stalks/ribs, cut on an angle into 2-cm/¾-in slices

4 tablespoons red wine vinegar

a 400-g/14-oz. can chopped tomatoes

2 teaspoons caster/granulated sugar

35 g/⅓ cup green olives, pitted and halved

1 tablespoon capers, rinsed and drained

20 g/¼ cup flaked/slivered almonds, lightly toasted

sea salt and freshly ground black pepper

a handful of flat-leaf parsley, to serve

GRILLED POLENTA

200 g/1⅓ quick-cook polenta/cornmeal

80 g/5 tablespoons butter

50 g/1 cup grated Parmesan

WHIPPED FETA

250 g/2 cups feta

60 ml/¼ cup Greek yogurt

60 ml/¼ cup extra virgin olive oil

1 tablespoon freshly squeezed lemon juice

an 18 x 25-cm/7 x 10-in baking pan, greased

a baking sheet, oiled

SERVES 6

Caponata is one of those dishes that improves with age and is extremely versatile. Served here with baked polenta, it makes a great vegetarian lunch or appetizer. It is also delicious as an accompaniment to grilled fish or chicken.

CAPONATA WITH GRILLED POLENTA & WHIPPED FETA

To make the caponata, place the aubergine/eggplant in a colander and sprinkle with salt. Leave for 30 minutes then rinse under cold, running water and pat dry with a kitchen towel.

Heat the oil in a large, heavy-bottomed saucepan or pot set over a medium heat. Add the aubergine/eggplant and fry for 5–8 minutes, until golden brown, stirring occasionally. Remove from the pan and set aside.

Add the onion to the same pan and fry for 5 minutes, or until softened. You may need to add a little more oil.

Add the garlic and cook for another minute before adding the peppers and celery. Cook for 5 minutes, then add the vinegar and stir to deglaze the pan.

Stir in the tomatoes and sugar and simmer for 5–10 minutes.

Return the aubergine/eggplant to the pan with the olives and capers, and mix well. Cook for a further 5 minutes. Remove from the heat, season and stir in the almonds.

To make the polenta, bring 1 litre/4 cups of salted water to the boil in a medium saucepan or pot. Gradually pour in the polenta while stirring continuously with a wooden spoon to prevent lumps forming.

Reduce the heat and keep stirring for about 5 minutes. Remove from the heat and stir in the butter and the Parmesan. Taste and adjust the seasoning as necessary.

Working quickly, spread the polenta mix evenly across the prepared baking pan to a layer 2 cm/¾ inch deep. Set aside to cool.

To make the Whipped Feta, crumble the feta into a food processor and pulse together with the yogurt until smooth. Add the oil and mix until it becomes very soft and spreadable. Add the lemon juice and set in the fridge.

Preheat a grill/broiler to a medium heat. Tip the set polenta onto a chopping board and cut into 6 rectangles. Then cut these in half diagonally to give you 12 triangles.

Place the polenta on the prepared baking sheet and set under the grill/broiler to cook for about 10 minutes, or until golden. Turn the polenta and grill the other side in the same way.

Reheat the caponata over a medium heat, add the chopped parsley and stir through. Heap the caponata onto a plate, top with the Grilled Polenta and a dollop of Whipped Feta. Sprinkle with pepper and serve with a green salad.

CAKES & BAKES

Upside-down fruit cakes are wonderfully simple as they don't need any frosting or other decoration. You just turn this one out onto a plate and reveal the beautiful glazed pineapple. This versatile recipe works well with other firm fruits like plums, apricots or pears too.

UPSIDE-DOWN PINEAPPLE & GINGER CAKE

100 g/scant $^1/_2$ cup clear honey
$^1/_2$ pineapple peeled, cored and cut into 1-cm/$^3/_8$-in wedges lengthways
300 g/2$^1/_2$ sticks butter
300 g/1$^1/_2$ cups caster/granulated sugar
4 eggs, lightly beaten
a 5-cm/2-in piece of fresh ginger, grated
grated zest of 2 lemons
200 g/1$^1/_4$ cups self-raising/rising flour
100 g/1$^1/_4$ cups shredded/desiccated coconut

a 23-cm/9-in round cake pan, greased and lined with baking parchment

SERVES 8

Preheat the oven to 180°C (350°F) Gas 4.

Pour the honey into the base of the cake pan. Top with the pineapple wedges in a fan shape. Set aside.

In a large mixing bowl, cream the butter and sugar together until light and fluffy. Gradually add the eggs and beat until combined. Add the grated ginger and lemon zest and stir to combine. Sift in the flour and fold in the coconut.

Pour the mixture over the pineapple and honey. Place the pan on a baking sheet and bake in the preheated oven for 45 minutes.

Reduce the oven temperature to 150°C (300°F) Gas 2 and continue to bake for 1 hour, until a skewer inserted into the middle comes out clean. If it looks as though the cake is getting too brown on top, cover with foil to stop it burning and return to the oven.

Remove the pan from the oven and transfer to a wire rack to cool for 2 minutes.

Slide a knife around the edge of the cake to loosen it. Place a serving plate over the top of the cake and carefully turn it out onto the plate. Replace any bits of pineapple that may have stuck to the pan and serve in thick slices.

This is a lovely moist cake which you could serve warm or cold with a cup of tea or coffee, or as an after-dinner dessert. Try substituting the pears for plums or rhubarb.

SPICED PEAR CAKE

250 g/2 cups plain/all-purpose flour

1½ teaspoons baking powder

1 teaspoon bicarbonate of/baking soda

1½ teaspoons ground cinnamon

1½ teaspoons ground ginger

2 large eggs

240 ml/1 cup milk

200 ml/scant 1 cup golden/light corn syrup

35 g/2 tablespoons clear honey

125 g/1 stick butter

125 g/⅔ cup light muscovado sugar

400 g/1½ cups (about 2 large) peeled, cored and sliced pears

6 tablespoons fruit preserve (apricot, apple or plum)

100 g/1 cup flaked/slivered almonds, toasted

a 23-cm/9-in round or 25-cm/10-in square cake pan, greased and lined with baking parchment

SERVES 6–8

Preheat the oven to 170°C (325°F) Gas 3.

Sift the flour, baking powder, bicarbonate of/baking soda, cinnamon and ginger into a large mixing bowl.

In a separate bowl, lightly whisk the eggs and milk together.

Warm the syrup, honey and butter very gently in a saucepan or pot set over a low heat. Stir in the sugar and keep on the heat until the butter and sugar melt together. Remove the pan from the heat and set aside to cool slightly.

Pour the warm syrup mixture into the bowl with the flour in and stir gently using a large, metal spoon. Add the whisked egg mixture and stir to combine.

Pour the mixture into the prepared cake pan and drop in the pear slices evenly over the surface – they should sink into the batter.

Bake in the preheated oven for 45–60 minutes, until a skewer inserted into the middle comes out clean, checking regularly after 40 minutes. If it looks as though the cake is getting too brown on top, cover with foil to stop it burning and return to the oven.

Meanwhile, melt the preserve in a saucepan or pot set over a medium heat.

Remove the cake from the oven and liberally brush with the warmed preserve while it is still warm. Sprinkle with flaked/slivered almonds and serve.

When I moved to London I discovered that the oval shaped cake pans that are used to bake friands in Australia are virtually impossible to buy in the UK. Many a time have I returned to London from holidays in Australia with a heavy suitcase filled with cake pans. Friands will actually taste exactly the same if you make them in round mini muffin pans but for me, a friand should always be oval.

BERRY FRIANDS

250 g/2 cups icing/
  confectioners' sugar
50 g/6 tablespoons
  plain/all-purpose
  flour
170 g/1¼ cups ground
  almonds
grated zest of 1 lemon
6 egg whites

200 g/1 stick plus 6
  tablespoons
  unsalted butter,
  melted
85 g/⅔ cup blueberries
85 g/⅔ cup raspberries

a 12-hole non-stick
  friand or muffin pan,
  well-greased

MAKES 12

Preheat the oven to 180°C (350°F) Gas 4.

Sift the icing/confectioners' sugar and flour into a large mixing bowl, then stir through the ground almonds and lemon zest.

In a separate bowl, lightly beat the egg whites with a whisk or fork to break them up, then stir them through the dry ingredients to make a smooth paste.

Add half of the melted butter to the batter and stir well before adding the remaining butter.

Fold in half of the blueberries and raspberries, then divide the batter evenly in the pan – they should be two-thirds full.

Place the remaining berries on top and bake in the preheated oven for 15–20 minutes, until firm and golden brown.

Remove the pan from the oven and let it cool on a wire rack for about 10 minutes before turning the friands out.

Serve hot or cold – either way they're delicious!

COFFEE CULTURE

Coffee is to Australians what bread is to the French. It is an integral part of daily life and most people can't function without their morning hit. It might seem an unlikely passion for a nation associated with warm weather and cold beer but Australians are proudly snobbish about their coffee and won't suffer a bad one lightly.

Cafés live and die by their coffee reputation. Customers will vote with their feet (and mouths) if a café doesn't source good beans, have skilled baristas and use proper coffee machines and equipment. It's not unusual for cafés to roast their own coffee or produce their own unique blend, as well as offer a number of different brew methods – pour-over, syphon, aeropress and of course, old school espresso.

Italian immigrants played a significant role in shaping Australia's coffee culture, bringing espresso coffee to its shores in the 1950s. For whatever reason, the expectation for good-quality espresso became firmly entrenched in the mindset of Australian coffee drinkers. This has inevitably fostered the growth of independent cafés, coffee houses and artisan roasters across cities, suburbs and coastal towns to the extent that attempts by the corporate chains to establish a foothold on the Australian high street have, so far, famously failed.

You're unlikely to remember the exact time and place you tried your first great coffee. But no doubt you remember the ensuing frustration in trying to recapture that 'espresso moment'. Why doesn't every coffee have that perfect bittersweet balance and heady aroma? Luckily, today, good coffee is not so hard to find if you know where to look.

The 'flat white' is perhaps the most famous Antipodean style of coffee – I say Antipodean as it is hotly contested whether Australians or New Zealanders created the flat white. It is an espresso-based coffee with milk, made with a double shot in a 170-ml/ 6-oz. cup and typically adorned with a latte art rosetta. Its been exported around the world by Australian and New Zealand expatriates who (like me) have opened cafés and coffee shops as a way of ensuring that they can get good coffee. Ironically, now even the big coffee chains have flat whites on their menus in an attempt to prove their coffee credentials. They're not fooling anyone.

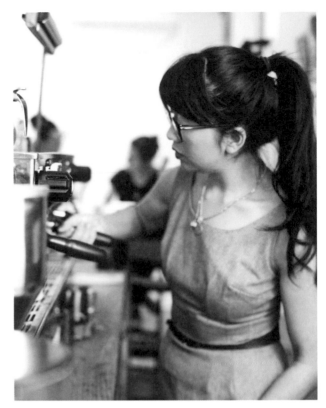

'Banana, pineapple, cinnamon, pecans with a cream cheese frosting,' has become a mantra for staff at our cafés. It is the automated response to one of the questions most frequently asked by customers: 'What is a crack cake?' While these cakes may look sweet and innocent, they are the most lusted after and fought over item on the cake counter. Lusted after, because you know that the quantity of frosting cannot be good for you, so you deny yourself the indulgence of eating one every day. Fought over because our chefs can't bake and ice them as fast as we can sell them.

CRACK CAKES

150 g/1 cup plus 3 tablespoons plain/all-purpose flour
75 g/²⁄₃ cup self-raising/rising flour
½ teaspoon bicarbonate of/baking soda
½ teaspoon baking powder
½ teaspoon ground cinnamon
½ teaspoon ground coriander
220 g/1 cup light brown sugar
50 g/²⁄₃ cup shredded/desiccated coconut
50 g/¹⁄₃ cup chopped pecans
180 ml/³⁄₄ cup sunflower oil
2 eggs, lightly beaten
2 ripe bananas, mashed
300 g/1½ cups drained crushed pineapple
shredded/dessicated coconut or pecan, to garnish (optional)

FROSTING
175 g/³⁄₄ cup cream cheese
120 g/1 stick unsalted butter, softened
440 g/3½ cups icing/confectioners' sugar
a few drops of pure vanilla extract

a 12-hole muffin pan lined with 12 paper cases

MAKES 12

Preheat the oven to 170°C (325°F) Gas 3.

Sift the flours, bicarbonate of/baking soda, baking powder and spices into a large mixing bowl. Add the sugar, coconut and pecans, and stir to combine.

In a separate bowl, mix the oil and whisked eggs together.

Put the drained pineapple in a food processor and pulse to fine pieces. Place the fruit in a fine mesh sieve/strainer and press out any excess moisture.

Add the strained pineapple to the oil mixture with the mashed banana, then pour into the dry ingredients. Stir gently to combine but do not beat the mixture.

Divide the mixture evenly between the paper cases. Bake in the preheated oven for 25–30 minutes, until a skewer inserted into a cake comes out clean. Remove the pan from the oven and set the cakes on a wire rack to cool.

To make the frosting, place the cream cheese, butter, icing/confectioners' sugar and vanilla in a freestanding electric mixer and beat until smooth.

Spread the frosting on top of the cooled cakes and garnish with coconut or pecans, if desired.

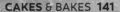

120 g/1 cup self-
raising/rising flour
70 g/1 scant cup
shredded/desiccated
coconut
75 g/⅓ cup caster/
granulated sugar
110 g/7 tablespoons
unsalted butter,
melted

CARAMEL
1 x 395-g/14-oz. can
sweetened
condensed milk
120 g/1 stick unsalted
butter
120 g/½ cup soft light
brown sugar
100 g/⅔ cup roasted
salted peanuts,
roughly chopped

TOPPING
150 g/1¼ cups chopped
dark/bittersweet
chocolate
100 ml/scant ½ cup
double/heavy cream
coarse sea salt, to
decorate (optional)

a 20 x 30-cm/8 x 12-in
baking pan, greased
and lined with baking
parchment

SERVES 20–24

This treat brings back the wonder of childhood when you discovered that boiling a can of condensed milk created caramel. The salted peanuts help to cut through its intense sweetness and add a lovely crunch.

CHOCOLATE & SALTED CARAMEL PEANUT SLICE

Preheat the oven to 180°C (350°F) Gas 4.

Place the flour, coconut and caster/granulated sugar in a large mixing bowl. Pour the melted butter over the dry ingredients, mix together and press firmly into the base of the prepared baking pan.

Bake in the preheated oven for about 15 minutes, or until light golden in colour. Remove from the oven and set aside to cool.

To make the caramel layer, place the unopened can of condensed milk on a folded kitchen towel in a deep saucepan or pot to stop it rattling while it boils. Cover completely with warm water, bring to the boil over a medium–high heat. Reduce the heat to low and simmer for 4 hours.

Remove from the water and allow the can to cool before opening it – the milk will have magically transformed into caramel.

In a separate saucepan or pot set over a medium heat, melt the butter with the light brown sugar, until the sugar has completely dissolved. Add the cooked condensed milk, reduce the heat and simmer for 10 minutes until the mixture has thickened slightly.

Pour the hot caramel mixture over the baked base and sprinkle the salted peanuts evenly across the top.

To make the topping, melt the chocolate and cream together in a heatproof bowl set over a pan of simmering water, making sure the base of the bowl doesn't touch the water below. Pour evenly over the caramel layer and chill in the fridge.

Once set, remove from the fridge and sprinkle with coarse sea salt. Cut into even square slices and serve stacked high on a plate.

There is always at least one gluten-free cake on the counter at the café and this is one of my favourite. I don't think the fact that it is flourless has anything to do with its popularity – it's just a delicious lemony treat.

LEMON POLENTA CAKE

200 g/1 stick plus 6 tablespoons butter
230 g/1 cup plus 2½ tablespoons golden caster/raw cane sugar
3 eggs
200 g/1⅓ cups ground almonds
100 g/¾ cup polenta/cornmeal
1 teaspoon baking powder
3 lemons

LEMON ICING
1 tablespoon freshly squeezed lemon juice
250 g/2 cups icing/confectioners' sugar

6 x 170-ml/6-oz. pudding moulds, greased and base-lined with a small circle of baking parchment

MAKES 8

Preheat the oven to 170°C (325°F) Gas 3.

Beat the butter and 200 g/1 cup of the sugar together in a large mixing bowl, until light and fluffy. Add the eggs, one at a time, beating well after each addition. Add small amounts of ground almonds if the mixture begins to curdle. Add in the remaining ground almonds and beat well. Stir in the polenta/yellow cornmeal and baking powder. Add the grated zest and freshly squeezed juice of ½ a lemon and stir again.

Divide the batter evenly between the prepared pudding moulds and put them on a baking sheet. Bake in the preheated oven for 20 minutes or until a skewer inserted into a cake comes out clean.

Meanwhile, make a lemon syrup. Place the zest and juice of the remaining lemons in a saucepan set over a gentle heat, with the remaining sugar. Stir to combine and heat until the sugar has dissolved completely.

Remove the cakes from the oven and prick all over with a skewer. Pour the lemon syrup over each cake and let it soak through – about 1 tablespoon per cake.

Let cool in the pudding basins for 15 minutes before turning the cakes out to cool completely.

To make the Lemon Icing, add just enough lemon juice to the icing/confectioners' sugar for a thick but slightly runny consistency.

When ready to serve, spoon the lemon icing on top of cakes and let it drip down their sides.

Part cake, part pudding; the complete package. Serve thick slices of this apple and blackberry cake with cream.

APPLE & BLACKBERRY STREUSEL CAKE

220 g/1¾ cups plain/
  all-purpose flour
½ teaspoon
  bicarbonate of/
  baking soda
1 teaspoon baking
  powder
a pinch of salt
85 g/6 tablespoons
  unsalted butter,
  at room temperature
140 g/¾ cup
  granulated/white
  sugar
2 large eggs
1 teaspoon pure vanilla
  extract
200 ml/¾ cup sour/
  soured cream

FILLING
450 g/4½ cups peeled,
  cored and quartered
  Granny Smith apples
2 tablespoons caster/
  granulated sugar
150 g/1 generous cup
  fresh blackberries

TOPPING
80 g/⅓ cup light brown
  sugar
1 teaspoon ground
  cinnamon
a pinch of ground
  cloves
35 g/3 tablespoons
  granulated/white
  sugar
40 g/⅓ cup plain/
  all-purpose flour
a pinch of salt
40 g/1½ tablespoons
  butter, cubed
20 g/2½ tablespoons
  chopped pecans

a 20-cm/8-in round
  cake pan, greased
  and lined with baking
  parchment
SERVES 8–10

Begin by making the apple filling. Combine the chopped apples with the sugar and 3 tablespoons water in a medium saucepan or pot. Set over a medium–high heat and bring to the boil. Reduce the heat, cover and simmer for about 5 minutes, until the apple is tender. Stir through the blackberries and set aside.

Next, prepare the streusel topping. Combine the light brown sugar, cinnamon and cloves in a medium mixing bowl. Stir in the granulated/white sugar, flour and salt. Add the cubed butter and rub into the mixture using your fingertips, until you have a crumbly texture. Stir in the pecans, cover and set in the freezer until ready to use.

Preheat the oven to 170°C (325°F) Gas 3.

Sift the flour, bicarbonate of/baking soda, baking powder and salt into a large mixing bowl.

In a separate bowl, cream the butter and sugar together until light and fluffy. Add the eggs and vanilla and beat until combined.

Add half of the flour mixture and half the sour/soured cream to the egg mixture and stir gently with a spatula until just combined. Repeat with the remaining flour and sour cream.

Spread one-third of the mixture evenly over the base of the prepared cake pan. Top with the apple and blackberry filling. Spoon the remaining cake mixture on top and smooth over the surface with a palette knife.

Sprinkle the streusel topping evenly over the surface of the cake and bake in the preheated oven for 55 minutes, until golden on top and a skewer inserted into the middle comes out clean, remembering that there will be some moisture from the fruit centre but the batter should be cooked through.

Remove from the oven and serve warm or cold, cut into slices.

While we don't try to do anything too blatantly 'Aussie', this bake is a tribute to an iconic Australian chocolate bar. Whether you're Australian or not, cherry and dark chocolate is a killer combination. Fair dinkum.

CHERRY RIPE SLICE

140 g/1 stick plus 2 tablespoons butter, melted

315 g/10½ oz. plain tea biscuits/cookies or vanilla wafers, crushed

1 tablespoon cocoa powder

FILLING

750 g/4 cups glacé cherries

125 ml/½ cup condensed milk

150 g/1 generous cup shredded/desiccated coconut

1½ teaspoons pure vanilla extract

TOPPING

150 g/1¼ cups chopped dark/bittersweet chocolate

100 ml/scant ½ cup double/heavy cream

50 g/⅓ cup white chocolate, to decorate

a 20 x 30-cm/8 x 12-in baking pan, greased and lined with baking parchment

SERVES 20–24

Preheat the oven to 180°C (350°F) Gas 4.

Put the melted butter, biscuits/cookies and cocoa powder in a food processor and pulse to a fine crumb. Press firmly into the base of the prepared baking pan.

For the filling, put 600 g/3⅓ cups of the glacé cherries into a food processor and blitz to a fine mince. Add the condensed milk, coconut and vanilla and pulse until smooth. Roughly chop the remaining cherries and stir them through the mixture. Spread evenly over the biscuit base.

Bake in the preheated oven for 25 minutes, or until starting to firm up and turn golden. Remove from the oven and set aside to cool completely.

To make the topping, melt the dark/bittersweet chocolate and cream together in a heatproof bowl set over a pan of simmering water, making sure the base of the bowl doesn't touch the water below.

Pour evenly over the cooled slice. Chill in the fridge until the topping has set.

Melt the white chocolate as above and then drizzle the melted chocolate across the slice using a teaspoon.

Return to the fridge to chill until the drizzle has set and then cut into even squares.

These are particularly delicious enjoyed with a spicy chai latte.

Sometimes you can have your cake and pudding too. This recipe combines two delicious desserts, sticky toffee pudding and ginger cake, into one decadent treat.

STICKY TOFFEE GINGER LOAF

200 g/1⅓ cups pitted dates, halved

1 teaspoon bicarbonate of/baking soda

75 g/5 tablespoons unsalted butter, softened

115 g/½ cup soft brown sugar

2 teaspoons ground ginger

3 eggs

80 g/½ cup (about 4 balls) stem ginger, finely chopped

225 g/1¾ cups self-raising/rising flour, sifted

CARAMEL GLAZE

110 g/½ cup caster/granulated sugar

40 g/3 tablespoons butter

225 ml/1 scant cup single/light cream

a 900-g/2-lb loaf pan, greased and lined with baking parchment

SERVES 6–8

Preheat the oven to 180°C (350°F) Gas 4.

Place the dates and bicarbonate of/baking soda in a large mixing bowl. Cover with 330 ml/1⅓ cups of boiling water. Stir and set aside for at least 20 minutes.

In a separate bowl, beat the butter and sugar together until thick and pale in colour. Add the ground ginger, then the eggs, one at a time, beating well after each addition.

Stir in the soaked date mixture, stem ginger and flour, and mix until well combined – the mixture should be quite loose.

Pour the batter into the prepared pan and bake in the preheated oven for 50–60 minutes, until a skewer comes out clean.

Remove from the oven and let the cake cool in the pan for 10 minutes, then turn out onto a wire rack to cool completely.

To make the Caramel Glaze, choose a saucepan or pot large enough to ensure that the sugar is no more than 2 mm/⅛ inch thick over the base, otherwise the heat will not distribute evenly through the sugar. Set the pan over a gentle heat and add the sugar and 1 teaspoon of water. Shake the pan rather than stir it with a spoon to avoid the sugar hardening before it liquifies – this will take about 15 minutes and you want a deep, golden caramel. Remove from the heat and whisk in the butter until it has all melted and is well combined.

Heat the cream in a separate saucepan or pot set over a gentle heat, then whisk it into the caramel until smooth and glossy. Set aside to cool and firm up slightly so that it has a good spreading consistency.

Spread the glaze over the top of the cooled cake and serve in slices.

Nothing says Australian summer to me quite like pavlova. Crisp meringue with a soft marshmallowy centre, it's bright and bold, generous, unrefined, and always a crowd-pleaser.

PAVLOVA WITH STRAWBERRIES & PASSION FRUIT CURD

6 egg whites

a pinch of salt

375 g/2 cups caster/ superfine sugar

3 teaspoons cornflour/ cornstarch

1½ teaspoons white wine vinegar

½ teaspoon pure vanilla extract

PASSION FRUIT CURD

4 passion fruit

1 large egg, plus 2 large egg yolks

115 g/½ cup plus 1 tablespoon caster/ granulated sugar

75 g/5 tablespoons unsalted butter

1 teaspoon freshly squeezed lime juice

TOPPING

500 ml/2 cups whipping/heavy cream

5 passion fruit

300 g/3 cups fresh strawberries, hulled and halved

SERVES 6–8

Begin by making the Passion Fruit Curd. Place the pulp of the passion fruit in a food processor and blitz to loosen the seeds. Strain into a jug/pitcher using a fine mesh sieve/strainer.

Put the egg and egg yolks in a medium mixing bowl and whisk to combine. Set aside.

Put the butter with the sugar and strained passion fruit juice in a small heavy-bottomed saucepan or pot set over a gentle heat, and stir until the butter has melted and the sugar has dissolved.

Pour one-third of the butter mixture into the whisked eggs, then return to the pan.

Continue to cook gently, stirring continuously with a wooden spoon, until the mixture has thickened and coats the back of the spoon. It is important not to let the mixture get too hot as it will scramble the eggs and may curdle.

Remove from the heat and stir through the lime juice and the pulp of the remaining passion fruit.

Press a piece of clingfilm/plastic wrap onto the surface of the curd to prevent a skin forming and set in the fridge for 1 hour, or until chilled.

Preheat the oven to 180°C (350°F) Gas 4.

Draw a 25-cm/10-inch diameter circle onto a piece of baking parchment, then turn the paper over and place on a baking sheet.

In a clean, dry bowl, whisk the egg whites and salt to soft peaks. Add the sugar, one-third at a time, whisking after each addition until the peaks become stiff and shiny.

Sprinkle the cornflour/ cornstarch, vinegar and vanilla over the whisked whites, and gently fold until just combined.

Heap the meringue onto the baking parchment within the marked circle and use a large spoon or spatula to flatten the top and shape it into a round circle.

Place in the preheated oven and immediately reduce the heat to 150°C (300°F) Gas 2. Cook for 1¼ hours, then turn off the oven and leave the meringue to cool completely in the oven.

For the topping, whisk the cream until just whipped, then fold through half of the chilled passion fruit curd.

Turn the pavlova over onto a plate and peel off the baking parchment. Turn back over then spoon the passion fruit cream onto the meringue base. Layer with more passion fruit curd and top with fresh passion fruit pulp and strawberries.

225 g/1¾ cups plain/
all-purpose flour
2 tablespoons icing/
confectioners' sugar
110 g/1 stick butter,
cubed
1 egg
a pinch of salt
clotted cream, to serve

TOPPING
100 g/½ cup caster/
granulated sugar
grated zest of 1 orange
½ teaspoon pure
vanilla extract
5–6 ripe plums,
stoned/pitted and
cut into sixths

FILLING
250 g/2 sticks plus
1 tablespoon
unsalted butter
250 g/1¼ cups caster/
granulated sugar
2 large eggs
250 g/1¾ cups ground
almonds
30 g/¼ cup flaked/
slivered almonds

a 28-cm/11-in round,
deep, fluted tart pan
baking beans

SERVES 8

Frangipane is a sweet almond filling that can be used as a base for many delicious tarts. We use whatever fruit is in season at the café; figs, berries, rhubarb or even just raspberry preserve to make a classic British bakewell tart.

PLUM FRANGIPANE TART

Preheat the oven to 190°C (375°F) Gas 5.

To make the pastry case, sift the flour and sugar into a large mixing bowl. Tip the cubed butter into the bowl and rub together with your fingertips to fine breadcrumbs.

In a jug/pitcher or small bowl, beat the egg together with 1 tablespoon of ice-cold water. Pour into the flour mixture with the salt and slowly bring the ingredients together.

Turn out onto a lightly floured surface and knead the dough lightly. Wrap the dough in clingfilm/ plastic wrap and chill in the fridge for at least 30 minutes, until firm.

Roll the dough out as thinly as possible on a lightly floured surface. Line the tart pan with the pastry and prick the base all over with a fork.

Place the pan on a baking sheet, line with a piece of greased baking parchment larger than the pan and fill the case with baking beans.

Bake in the preheated oven for 15 minutes. Remove the baking beans and return the pan to the oven for 5 minutes, until pale golden.

Reduce the heat to 170°C (325°F) Gas 3.

To make the plum topping, put the sugar, orange zest and vanilla with 450 ml/2 cups of water in a saucepan or pot set over a medium heat. Bring to a simmer, add the plums and lower the heat. Poach the plums for 3–4 minutes, then strain and discard the liquid.

For the frangipane filling, beat the butter and sugar together in a large mixing bowl until light and fluffy. Crack the eggs into the bowl, one at a time, beating well after each addition. Add the ground almonds and mix, until combined.

Spoon the filling into the pastry case, smooth over the surface with a spatula and cover evenly with the poached plums. Scatter flaked/ slivered almonds on top and bake in the still-warm oven for 45 minutes, or until the pastry is crisp and the fruit is tender.

Remove from the oven and serve hot or cold, cut into slices, with clotted cream.

The honey–orange syrup on this cake helps to keep it lovely and moist, but it is still best eaten the day it is made.

ORANGE & HONEY CAKE

170 g/1 stick plus
    4 tablespoons
    unsalted butter
340 g/1¾ cups caster/
    granulated sugar
3 large eggs
2 teaspoons grated
    orange zest, plus
    extra to decorate
1½ teaspoons pure
    vanilla extract
300 ml/1¼ cups sour/
    soured cream
375 g/3 cups plain/
    all-purpose flour
2 teaspoons baking
    powder
½ teaspoon
    bicarbonate of/
    baking soda
a pinch of salt

SYRUP
100 g/scant ½ cup
    clear honey
100 ml/⅓ cup orange
    juice
1–2 tablespoons orange
    blossom water

TOPPING
85 g/6 tablespoons
    butter, softened
250 g/2 cups icing/
    confectioners' sugar
1 teaspoon pure vanilla
    extract
1 tablespoon clear
    honey

a 23-cm/9-in round
    cake pan, greased
    and lined with baking
    parchment

SERVES 8

Preheat the oven to 170°C (325°F) Gas 3.

Cream the butter and caster/granulated sugar together in a large mixing bowl, until light and fluffy. Add the eggs, one at a time, then add the zest, vanilla and sour/soured cream.

In a separate bowl, sift the flour, baking powder, bicarbonate of/baking soda and salt. Gently fold into the butter mixture, until just combined.

Spoon the batter into the prepared cake pan and bake in the preheated oven for 50–60 minutes, or until the cake is springy to the touch and a skewer inserted into the middle comes out clean.

Meanwhile, make an orange syrup. Place the honey and orange juice in a saucepan or pot set over a gentle heat, with 150 ml/⅔ cup of water. Simmer for 5 minutes to reduce the syrup by half. Stir in the orange blossom water and remove from the heat.

Remove the cake from the oven and prick all over with a skewer. Pour over the orange syrup and let it soak through. Place on a wire rack to cool completely in the pan.

To make the topping, place the butter and icing/confectioners' sugar in a freestanding electric mixer and beat on a low speed, until combined. Increase the speed and beat for 3 minutes. Add the vanilla and honey and continue to beat for 1 minute, until smooth.

When the cake is completely cool, spread the topping over the cake and decorate with a little extra orange zest.

INDEX

ACKNOWLEDGMENTS

I know I will pinch myself every time I see the Lantana cookbook sitting on my kitchen shelf beside books written by all of my food heroes. Thank you to the team at Ryland Peters & Small for reassuring me that the world needs another cookbook and for holding my hand as I wrote it.

To our wonderful customers, this book is for you. Now stop pestering me for recipes.

Thank you to the entire Lantana team but especially the chefs, past and present, who have been instrumental in the success of the cafés and who have helped develop many of these recipes. George Notley, Tim Dorman, Adam Shepherd and Lisa Creigh; you have all left an indelible mark on Lantana and I admire you immensely.

To Michael Homan, my business partner and brother-in-law, thank you for allowing me to focus on the fun stuff while you sharpen the pencils and keep the business running. Who says family members can't work together?

To Mat, I always knew you had impeccable taste but in the process of writing this book I've discovered that you have many hidden talents; proofreader, food critic, recipe tester and cheerleader. Thank you.

To little Vinnie, always a welcome distraction.

Lastly, thank you to my dad, who nurtured my love of eating and cooking and taught me the art of being a good host. I wish you had been able to see Lantana. I think you would approve.

ACKNOWLEDGMENTS

I know I will pinch myself every time I see the Lantana cookbook sitting on my kitchen shelf beside books written by all of my food heroes. Thank you to the team at Ryland Peters & Small for reassuring me that the world needs another cookbook and for holding my hand as I wrote it.

To our wonderful customers, this book is for you. Now stop pestering me for recipes.

Thank you to the entire Lantana team but especially the chefs, past and present, who have been instrumental in the success of the cafés and who have helped develop many of these recipes. George Notley, Tim Dorman, Adam Shepherd and Lisa Creigh; you have all left an indelible mark on Lantana and I admire you immensely.

To Michael Homan, my business partner and brother-in-law, thank you for allowing me to focus on the fun stuff while you sharpen the pencils and keep the business running. Who says family members can't work together?

To Mat, I always knew you had impeccable taste but in the process of writing this book I've discovered that you have many hidden talents; proofreader, food critic, recipe tester and cheerleader. Thank you.

To little Vinnie, always a welcome distraction.

Lastly, thank you to my dad, who nurtured my love of eating and cooking and taught me the art of being a good host. I wish you had been able to see Lantana. I think you would approve.